*Crossing*

"As much as I admire Warren Smith as a musician, I find even deeper resonance with his fierce and abiding love of and commitment to family. And this articulates through his family and his extended family of colleagues, students, listeners, and the commoner. Warren has taught me much, directly and through example, about love and caring for others. What does this have to do with the music? All of this has everything to do with the music. A powerful love energy informs and infuses Warren's work. Important to understand and learn from that, as well. And let's not forget Warren's laughter! There are abundant lessons to be had in the apprehension of that particular healing force and how Warren consistently and generously deploys it."
—*Stephen Haynes, trumpeter, composer, music teacher*

"The author of this book is a world traveler whose career has extended for over 65 years. Warren shares his talent and success with those he loves. He provided for his family and created a place for himself and others in the highly competitive world capital of music, New York City. Warren Smith's training, skill, talent, and humility, along with his dedication to physical conditioning, have made it possible for his unique talent to flourish. Long live WIS!" —*Maurice McKinley, Drummer, Executive Director of the Uhuru Jazz and Literacy Program*

"Throughout the history of civilization, the drum has served as a vital form of human communication. In traditional West

African cultures, those so expert in the craft of speaking and motivating through percussion are bestowed with the title of "Master Drummer." Warren Smith is a Master Drummer. In addition to being a musician of prodigious versatility, in collaboration with Max Roach and their ground-breaking ensemble, M'Boom, or as a session player or pit drummer for Broadway shows, Smith is a highly respected educator who has taught the essence of music history by being the essence of music history. When you hear the polyrhythms of contemporary jazz or the syncopated funk breakbeats that became the sonic foundation for hip-hop, you're hearing the influences of the legendary Warren Smith."

*—Bill Stephney, music producer, Public Enemy; executive member, Smithsonian Anthology of Hip-Hop and Rap*

"As an original member of the Untempered Ensemble, which I founded in the 1990s, Warren Smith has played on all 18 CDs I produced for the band. I first met him at a jazz seminar at the University of Pittsburgh in 1970. We were both visitors. He was so friendly and positive. Little did I know we would go on to be music associates and good friends for all these years. I also didn't know what an experienced musician he was, having played in every possible situation a percussionist could play in: Broadway shows, accompanying famous singers like Barbara Streisand, Nina Simone, Janis Joplin, Aretha Franklin, as well as symphony orchestras and jazz bands. I've seen his group, Composer's Workshop Ensemble, at Studio WIS, a performance space on West 21st Street in Chelsea. He can play the timpani, set kit, balafon, marimba, xylophone, gong—anything with sticks and a cover. An excellent composer and arranger, he is a musician's musician." —*Bill Cole, multi-instrumentalist, ethnomusicologist, professor of African American Studies*

"I can truly say that I owe Warren Smith my life. I met Warren in 1981. Eventually he asked me to help him out with Sunday music classes for the kids that were held at Studio WIS. From these classes, Warren told me that I was a natural teacher, and that if I ever wanted to raise a family, own a house and have a comfortable lifestyle I should go into teaching like him. The plan he laid out was that I go back to school, get my music degree at SUNY/Old Westbury (where he was a professor), then go on to get my master's in education at Queens College. By the time I got my master's degree he would be ready to retire and I would take over his position at the university as the percussion teacher. Well, things didn't work out quite as planned; the music department was terminated by the powers that be. I got a position as head of the music department in one of the top high schools in NYC, and now I am two years out of retirement. I have a house, a beautiful family and still continue my musical career just as my mentor, friend and bandmate WIS laid out for me all those years ago. God bless Warren Smith." —*Lloyd Haber*

"Warren showed me the blueprint of how to be a successful performing musician-composer and a respected community member. He also guided me on how to succeed in academia and life in general. Always affable, he makes you feel good about what you are supposed to do and that no matter what happens, everything will be all right." —*Dr. William E. Smith, Associate Professor of Music Technology, Bowie State University.*

# CROSSING BORDERS AND PLAYING WITH PIONEERS: MY LIFE IN MUSIC

*by Warren I. Smith*

Warren I. Smith
Crossing Borders and Playing with Pioneers: My Life in Music



Grateful acknowledgment to the Taking Giant Steps Press blog, where earlier versions of some tales were published.

Smith, Warren, I., 1934-
Crossing Borders and Playing with Pioneers: My Life in Music
Summary: The life and times of legendary jazz drummer and percussionist Warren I. Smith, from early influences, through the Chicago and New York Jazz scenes, to an impressive career with some of the century's most legendary performers.

**ISBN: 979-8-9889824-0-1 (eBook)**
**ISBN: 979-8-9889824-1-8 (Print)**

*Cover art by Frank Smith*
*Cover design by Code Cherry Designs*
*Book design by Tabetha Hedrick*

First Edition

*I wish to dedicate my story to my family: my wife, Debby Randolph; my five daughters: Lynn, Leslie, Mikey, Stephanie, and Nairobi; and my second wife Patricia. I wish to let them all know how much they and my deceased first wife, Mary Carmen Scott, have influenced my life and my professional career as an educator and performer. They have all helped make my accomplishments possible and given me the support I needed to make my efforts worthwhile.*

*I also wish to thank my brother, Frank Evans Smith, for always being at my side whenever I needed him. As we used to say, "From the cradle to the grave." I'll be here for him as long as I am able. My family is my life, and my closest friends are and always have been a part of my family.*

# *Contents*

# PART 1

## *Sweet Home, Chicago, 1934-1957*

# CHAPTER 1

## *Moonglow, Frank & the Family Band*

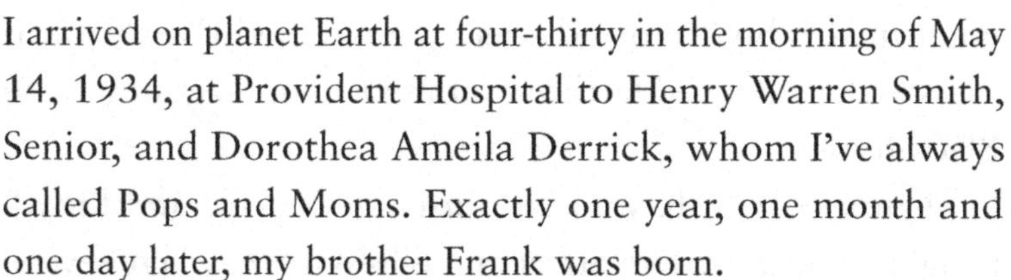

I arrived on planet Earth at four-thirty in the morning of May 14, 1934, at Provident Hospital to Henry Warren Smith, Senior, and Dorothea Ameila Derrick, whom I've always called Pops and Moms. Exactly one year, one month and one day later, my brother Frank was born.

Surrounded by a loving and musically gifted family in the all-Black world of Chicago's South Side, I was unaware the nation was still fighting its way through the Great Depression, that Prohibition had just been rescinded, and that marijuana was now illegal.

In pre-TV American society, radio ruled. For the first year or so, my frame of reference was "Moonglow," Duke Ellington's new hit song, which was all over the radio. It was the pacifier my mother and aunts used to quiet me. Moonglow became my nickname early on.

As for Chicago, man, it was fast, hip, intense—with music everywhere: dance halls, theaters, symphony spaces, nightclubs, blues joints, jam sessions. However, for all the many genres of music coming out of this widespread, slaughterhouse, meat-packing town, it remained the most rigidly segregated city north of the Mason-Dixon line.

Borders defined the real estate game in the Windy City. We lived south of the Loop between 12th Street and 31st Street, next to the Lakefront. As some knew only too well, a real estate phenomenon continually occurred when Black pioneers crossed a geographical border.

Such brazen audacity resulted in getting harassed and vandalized—that is to say, initially. When that method failed, what invariably followed was a "white flight" as Caucasian residents moved farther south to avoid integrating with Black folks.

Family rumor has it that our uncles, Steele and Lloyd, bought a house on 37th Street and Ellis Avenue, where several extended family members lived with our paternal grandfather, James Madison Smith. Someone set off a bomb in front of the house and blew out most of the windows. Frank and I were untouched, but broken glass embedded in the wall above our crib.

Our grandfather died not long after, his health certainly not helped by the neighborhood's "welcome." Other relatives had similar experiences as we gradually expanded farther south. But until I left for New York in 1957, that real estate phenomenon had not changed. Eventually, the violence stopped, at least the physical violence. As far as I know, things are quite different now for our next generation of cousins, at least geographically.

This Black segment of Chicago society felt completely empowered and pretty much self-sufficient. Although FDR's New Deal did not include many programs for African Americans, our segregation proved advantageous. We had our own school system with Black superintendents, principals, and associate principals. For context, let me add that I started teaching in "integrated" New York City in 1958. They got their first Black principal in 1966.

For more context, as Black musicians, we had our union with its credit union. The first building the Union owned was on State Street at 40th Street. When urban renewal caused that whole neighborhood to be torn down, the Union bought another building on Cottage Grove and 61st Street. And the Union owned an apartment on Drexel Boulevard in Hyde Park, which afforded many members an affordable home during trying times. Many of these resources were lost to us when the American Federation of Musicians integrated Local 208 with the white Union Local 10 and became the present Local 10-208.

Chicago's South Side has retained its power as a thriving Black community. It was so much that way during my youth that I rarely ventured outside of it except to go to school. I joined the musicians' union at age fourteen. I played music in church, social affairs, parades, and summer concerts. I didn't realize there was a Local 10 until I was twenty-one.

At home, music—ranging from pop to blues to jazz to symphony—continually permeated the environment. I couldn't have escaped music even if I tried. I was born into an orchestra! Pops played saxophone and clarinet. Moms played piano and harp; Frank and I often awoke to the sound of her harp. All our aunts and uncles were musicians and were always preparing to perform somewhere.

For the most part, all my relatives worked. Male relatives seemed to gravitate to post office employment and played music every night. They were doing what was essentially a Broadway-format show in a pit orchestra or performing in a nightclub where there were radio broadcasts. Frank and I heard some of them on the radio, either playing or singing along with well-known orchestras.

Often, even as infants, we went along to drop them off or pick them up. Sometimes we were allowed to come inside and see what was going on. I'm talking live theater with full orchestras, dancers, singers, and stage lighting. You can't imagine how early this captured my imagination. I was privileged to see the inside of Club DeLisa, the Grand Terrace, Tony's, and other fabled nightspots, holding Moms' coattails because Pops, uncles, and cousins were playing in the band.

One of the most exciting times was when one of the bands got ready to go on the road. Maybe they had a three-week engagement in Detroit or six weeks in Buffalo. The morning of their departure, women cooked and prepared bags of food. Three or four cars lined up at the curb, all being cleaned and simonized, the white-walled tires painted with whitewash, a water-based paint. Then the musicians appeared, each dressed stylishly and sharper than the last. Finally, after all the loved ones got their hugs and kisses and the food bags were distributed in all the cars, the motors started up, and they'd be off to cheers from the crowd. Boy, how we young kids longed to go with them. We couldn't wait for them to come home and tell all the funny stories and strange adventures they had experienced.

Every once in a while, one of our special talents got the opportunity to go to New York City. Almost all the aspiring musicians from Chicago wanted to follow in the footsteps of their musical idols to the Big Apple, home of Harlem, USA. That seed, with its implicit promise of freedom, of boundaries broken and borders crossed, was planted early.

It was no accident that I decided to be a professional musician by age three. I started trying to play my father's saxophone at that time. In a couple of years, I played what I could think of by ear. Pops was among the best teachers in Chicago, but why ask him? Thinking I knew more than I actually did resulted in many humbling moments. That was the price for being precocious, and I was no better when I started to tinker around with the piano. Moms and no fewer than three aunts had bachelor's degrees in piano and organ, but I never thought to consult them. I just did it by ear. My folks were wise enough to let me find my way.

One day when I was six years old, I went into a club called the Rhumboogie with Moms and Frank to pick up Pops from his gig. The ballroom was on the second floor. When we entered, I immediately saw a scene that changed my life: in the corner of the stage, the drummer had a set of flashing lights inside his bass drum. I decided on the spot to become a drummer. When I told my father, he found me drum teachers who kicked my ass in a way he wouldn't.

Oliver S. Coleman was my beginning teacher who taught me how to sight read and analyze music scores. I was all of eight years old. He taught Walter Perkins, Thurman Parker, and almost every prominent jazz musician who came out of Chicago. He had a big apartment with ten to twelve students waiting to take a half-hour lesson. In other words, we were on stage the whole time. And the lessons weren't cheap. They cost a dollar and fifty cents (a quart of milk plus a loaf of bread cost only 25 cents).

I remember the lesson in which Mr. Coleman sent me home. He said, "Mr. Smith, you didn't practice this week. I'm not going to take your money." Of course, I caught hell on both ends, embarrassed to mess up in front of my peers and teacher and embarrassed to reveal to Mom that I failed to practice. After that, I took practicing seriously and stayed with Mr. Coleman for six years.

When I got good enough, I started playing in the family band. Its leader was my father.

But he's a chapter all to himself.

# CHAPTER 2

## *Pops, Paris & Sax Convention*

The kindest man I met in my entire life was my father, Pops.

With his fair complexion and his black hair wavy and straight, Pops probably could have "passed" if he wanted to. But that wasn't a part of our family attitude.

Pops grew up in rural North Carolina, thirty miles south of the Greensboro-Winston Salem-Highpoint Airport, smack dab in the middle of what would become the Golden Triangle with Charlotte and Durham. Pops' grandmother (my great-grandmother), Versilla Littlelow, had three children with John Sellers. Their child, Emma Nora Sellers, my grandmother, was light-skinned. Nora had eleven children with

James Madison Smith, all born on the family homestead in North Carolina, which housed my great-grandmother, my paternal grandparents, and their children. Many of Pops' siblings got involved with music. Pops became a saxophonist and taught his younger brother Faber and Moms' younger brother Frank Derrick II. They became professional sax players as well.

Music has played a part in all our lives. Although none of my five daughters are professional musicians, they all took piano lessons and can read music. My four oldest daughters sang in their elementary school choir. They often sang (in four-part harmony) and re-enacted scenes from Broadway shows for their friends who visited our home. John, my son by marriage to Debby Randolph, known as Jay Smooth, is the founder of the longest-running hip-hop radio show, *The Underground Railroad*. Smith family gatherings always include multi-generational entertainment.

From infancy, Frank and I have heard tales of the music life from Pops and the many friends who constantly visited our apartment on 58th Street. Pops told us of Black American jazz and blues musicians traveling throughout France, Germany, and Italy in the Twenties and Thirties. He narrated his own story of crossing borders and pioneering this music. It was the story of his generation as well.

In the mid-1920s, Pops came east to New York and boarded a transatlantic ship to entertain European audiences in the cities and resort areas craving our music. Although he learned just before his departure that the gig he was promised in Paris had fallen through, he left anyway. It turned out that one of the passengers on the ship was a professional boxer named Al Smith who needed a sparring partner to help him train for his contest in Europe. Pops took on the job to have enough money to sustain himself once he got to France.

There was a tradition at the dock in Calais that all the expatriates from America came out to see who was arriving and what resources they had brought with them. Pops had a suitcase full of stock arrangements—jazz and blues music from America. Pops' older brother, William Lloyd Garrison Smith, our Uncle Lloyd, owned a thriving music publishing business in Chicago.

Before there was Spotify, YouTube, and the digital age, before folks played CDs, tape cassettes, eight-tracks, records, and albums, there was sheet music. People "shopped" at a music publishing house to find new material. The publishing house hired musicians to perform (sing and play, sight reading) and "demonstrate" the music for customers. Uncle Lloyd's pianist was Clarence Williams, and his singer was a young Bessie Smith. Pops was in his teen years and learned the business working in Uncle Lloyd's publishing house. It was the ultimate environment for a musical education.

So when Pops disembarked with his saxophone and clarinet cases as well as a chest of Uncle Lloyd's charts, Black American musicians welcomed him. Pops stayed for five years.

While living in Paris, he toured Europe with various bands, including Noble Sissle. When I was ready to make my maiden voyage in 1969, Pops sat me down and taught me the French phrases I needed to get around on my own. Everything he told me proved useful to my survival.

Locally, the mob owned many of Chicago's nightclubs. Pops played with different groups, including the legendary Captain Dyad's Club Date Band and Jimmy Noone's Apex Club Orchestra, which recorded for Decca. While I was growing up, Pops was always doing two or three jobs, playing music at night while working as a postal carrier by day and teaching in the afternoons at home.

As soon as I showed an interest, he let me blow on his instruments, and I learned how to play the sax. Later, I became his intern, helping with repairs and making minor adjustments on the instruments of his clients and students. It was an excellent apprenticeship. Traveling musicians, as well as locals, often came by. Visitors like Art Tatum came to the house and played piano all night. Pops repaired Sonny Stitt's and (pre-bop) Charlie Parker's horns. Future sax greats Gene Ammons and Johnny Griffin were just a few years older than Frank and me; they came to my father for lessons. I didn't realize the importance of this at the time, but a legendary saxophone convention took place in our apartment, and I absorbed the whole scene. As for my fascination with drums, it grew from being an incessant tapper.

To put Pops in perspective, at one point, Gene Ammons ended up incarcerated at Joliet Prison. There were so many musicians locked up there that Jug started a band. He called my father and told him the instruments were a mess, so Pops came to the prison with his repair kit and fixed them. That's how he did things.

As for discipline, Pops never spanked us. Through these years, the actual disciplining of my brother and me fell to my mother, grandmother, or sometimes aunts. Rather than deliver punishment, he had a knack for adjusting my attitude. He allowed me to learn from my errors. Instead of telling me what to do, Pops provided me with different ways of looking at my mess. By not taking sides, he let me figure it out, which helped me to develop my critical thinking and problem-solving skills. He also managed to drop a little knowledge on me when I wasn't looking.

Seeing my confused and beleaguered young face, he might remark, "There are two things you can never tell a young man anything about."

"What's that, Pops?" I'd say, taking the bait.

"A woman or a fucked-up used car."

I laughed along with him, but months later—sometimes years later—his remark would come back and sting me, the first and second parts. His skill in delivering these life lessons was in his off-handed manner. I used the same tactic with my children.

Pops cultivated kindness; he saw no future in being mean to folks. He never bugged anyone about an overdue or unpaid bill. But he was also no one's fool. He once told me, "Never loan anybody anything you can't afford to give away."

I once watched him fix the horn of a well-known musical artist and then "loan" the cat the money to get his suit out of the cleaners to make his gig! Pops never brought up the incident, but upon observing his magnanimity in my early life, I resolved never to allow a financial debt or professional jealousy to affect my relationship with a friend or associate.

To see him on stage performing, teaching a student, or repairing a sax was to see a human being in the game more deeply than those around him. A tremendous inspiration to me and my ultimate role model, Pops understood the value of forgiveness and keeping his heart open. Like Duke Ellington once said, “Don’t you dare kneel to pray until you have forgiven everyone.”

In short, my father was an advanced moral being. That ought to be all I needed. But in walked Mr. Derrick, my maternal grandfather.

# CHAPTER 3

## *Dad, Touring the USA & Family Diplomacy*

The second kindest man I ever met was my grandfather, whom I called Dad.

Dad was John Frank Derrick, my mother's father. He grew up in the area around Southern Illinois and Kentucky. Everyone, including his wife (even at home), called him Mr. Derrick. He was rumored to be a second cousin of Chief Tecumseh, the great Shawnee warrior and intertribal leader. Having escaped at an early age from attempted enslavement, Dad became a chef for the Chicago and Northwestern Railroad.

He bought a big two-story house with a basement in Maywood, Illinois. It had a large side yard and a back yard that was like a garden of Eden: rows of vegetables, cultivated mainly by Pops, which produced most of the produce we ate daily; many cherry trees, a rhubarb bush, currants, and Dad's herb garden with mint and other medicinal plants. We had a well from which we drew water and a rain barrel for utilitarian purposes. We also raised chickens.

Maywood, twenty miles due west of the Loop, was adjacent to Oak Park and River Forest, a rather affluent area with many Frank Lloyd Wright prairie-style houses in the residential neighborhoods. Maywood extended from First Avenue in the east to 26th Avenue in the west and from St. Charles Road in the north to Madison Avenue in the south. All the Black people in the town lived between 10th and 14th Avenues. One wealthy businessman owned a nice home on the corner of 15th and Oak Street. The renowned scientist Dr. Percy Julian lived on the corner of 14th and Oak. A few years later, Dr. Julian had the temerity to move to Oak Park. Of course, in true Chicago style, his house got bombed.

Leafy Maywood was where Dad and my grandmother Tillitha Derrick, whom we called Ma, raised my mother, my Aunt Lowell, and my Uncle Frank. Their home education included performing as a chamber music ensemble: Aunt Lowell on the piano, Mom on the harp, and Uncle Frank on the violin. On some occasions, Dad played the piano.

Musical talent was abundant on both sides of my family. Thanks to Dad's diplomacy, the Derrick musical tradition joined forces with the Smith musical tradition. Here's the back story: Ma did not entirely approve of Moms' relationship with Pops. But when I was born, Dad detected an opportunity to break the impasse between his wife and daughter. As he foresaw and encouraged, Ma softened her attitude when her grandchildren became irresistible to her. Ma had a large hand in raising Frank and me.

Just like with Pops, we heard stories about Dad's adventures all over the country. His retirement package from the railroad included free travel anywhere in the continental United States. He made good use of the opportunity. I remember him in his nineties, traveling to New York City and Los Angeles to visit relatives.

The guy made colorful exclamations—"Great Gordon's Gin" or "Great God and little fishes"—unforgettable to me, like a line of poetry or a song title, during the rare times he might raise his voice. I never heard anyone say a bad word about him. He helped anyone whenever he could and never talked about it. That's how I was brought up. You were expected to help one another and not fuss over it. This world-traveled, highly intelligent man understood the spiritual facts of life and the value of kinship bonds. He told Mom many times, "Never let anyone be nicer to you than you are to them." I've long ago accepted that as a part of my philosophy.

I vividly remember his strong Native American features and his straight, jet-black hair that became streaked with gray but stayed mostly black to the end of his life. His skin was smooth and dark brown. His hooked-nose profile looked like the image on a nickel. And he had a generous black brush mustache. He smoked his pipe daily and walked around the neighborhood in Maywood until his last days.

Ma died of cancer at the end of my sophomore year in high school. She was 67. Dad was rumored to have been at least thirty years her senior. When he passed away three years later, he was over a hundred years old, but nobody knew how old exactly.

I am also grateful that Dad was always looking out. He intervened when he thought Ma was too severe with me. For a fuller context, I was a complete fuck-up. I was constantly testing the limits and had to learn everything the hard way. Dad consoled me. He forgave and forgot my transgressions, major or minor. Like my father, Dad saw my mistakes as an opportunity to learn. Perhaps that is how I developed patience when raising my own family. Now, being a grandfather (and great-grandfather), I can appreciate how much he taught me—often without saying a word.

I hope to live out the rest of my life honoring the humanity my father and maternal grandfather instilled in me. I know this to be true for my brother as well. We are not just their namesakes. Like them, we have become pioneers in our fields—Frank in the visual arts and me in the musical arts. Like them, we learned how to cross borders.

# CHAPTER 4

## *The South Side & the Carolina Homestead*

Frank and I grew up in the South Side and Maywood but weren't alone. In both places, we were surrounded by more than a dozen first, second, and third cousins. They were all like brothers and sisters. Close friends—both in the South Side and Maywood, as well as the many unofficial godfathers and godmothers—extended this list. Occasionally we brought home a friend who needed attention. In most cases, they were simply "adopted" by the family.

These relationships have endured over all these generations. Our family is still expanding, and all comers are welcome. This attests to the innate ability of a culturally aware household to educate each individual within that environment so that they can choose their associates and life companions wisely. That is not to say that every intimate relationship will succeed in close quarters. But if there is a breakup, the phenomenal thing about our family is that usually both partners in the separation stay involved socially with the family. Over a generation, everyone forgets why it happened. Of course, kids aren't going to give up their cousins, grandparents, aunts, and uncles.

All of us in this extended family lived together, often ate, slept, and frequently traveled from Chicago to North Carolina to visit the Smith family homestead. Call it James Madison Smith's forty acres, and there was a mule involved as well. The trips took several days. We left Chicago with enough food to last us until we got to Washington D.C. In the 1930s and '40s, we didn't know where we might get served (or abused), so we drove straight through to where we knew it was safe.

In D.C., we had relatives. We spent the night, resupplied our food bank, and drove the last five or six hours to the homestead. After a week or two, we piled back into the two or three-car caravan and traveled back to Chicago the same way. We did this annually until our paternal grandmother, Nora Sellers Smith, died at 103. We occasionally return for periodic reunions or meet at another hosting location every few years. Somehow the tradition is still intact.

In North Carolina, we raised pigs and grew peanuts. We walked down the red dirt road in the morning and picked wild berries and fruit from the trees and bushes for breakfast. Sometimes Frank, my cousin Ethan, and I brought back enough blueberries and blackberries for our aunts to make a couple of pies. We went fishing and cooked outside in a big kettle over an open fire. We cooked dandelion leaves as greens or used them in salads. Little was wasted in those days. The family harvested, preserved, and canned fruits and vegetables during the fall. We brewed dandelion wine and corn liquor and roasted "redskin peanuts," walnuts, pecans, and other foodstuffs. Although we grew up in Chicago's South Side, we drove down to the country every summer, on special occasions, and spent time at family gatherings.

It may have been part of my folks' generation or cultural exposure or a general distrust of the medical practices at the time, but except for measles, chicken pox, or something infectious, most ailments were treated at home. Some adult would go out to the yard and pick something, then come in and prepare it for your aches and pains, fevers, and woes. They always had castor oil, cod liver oil, camphor oil, and a bunch of ointments and poultices. They kept gauze and clean cloth around to wrap or bandage wounds. If you got sick, they had a remedy. Two generations—Dad and Ma and Pops and Moms—took care of us and all our cousins just fine.

Chicago's South Side was completely urban and paved with asphalt. We lived in a large six-room flat with one bathroom, a kitchen with a large pantry, and a wooden back porch. All the units in the three-story building had a wooden back porch. The building was L-shaped and had two entrances—Calumet Avenue and 58th Street. Porches faced the north and south alley between Calumet and Prairie

Avenues. The 'L' tracks went north to the Loop and south to 59th Street, where it turned west to Englewood or 61st Street, then east to Jackson Park and the beach.

On 58th Street, there was a blues club, three drug stores, one liquor store, and two bars that sold alcoholic beverages. Hence, there was always lots of activity. Frank and I sat in the window every evening before bedtime, listening to the music and watching the show. All kinds of crazy circumstances unfolded before our eyes. A man got robbed in the middle of the side street and had to walk naked—just his hat, shoes, and socks—onto the train station to catch the 26 home. We saw shootings, beatings, fights, car crashes, train wrecks, and ambulances evacuating body parts. It was an early lesson in truth proving stranger and more fascinating than fiction. As Mark Twain observed, "Truth is stranger than fiction, but it is because fiction is obliged to stick to possibilities; truth is not."

At any given time, there might have been as many as twelve people living in the apartment just grouped together. It was a kind of socialist way of living. That was how we survived. Our family would have one room in the back, and then another uncle and his wife and family would have another room with people transitioning back and forth.

I don't know how we shared the bathroom with that many people, but the cooking was usually a group thing. And it was quite celebratory. I remember rent parties where folks were charged 25 cents to come in. Moms had cooked a big pot of chitlins, which were cheap, but the smell was so bad that my brother and I never tasted any. We'd go to bed to escape the smell. I was an adult before I ever tasted chitlins, and I still don't like them. Sometimes my relatives hunted in the woods and brought back small game like deer. Moms and my aunts cooked that into an invariably delicious meal.

Tenants in the building were like family. Across the hall was Minnie Wilson and her daughter Grace. Minnie was pretty and dark-complexioned, as was Grace. The pharmacist Moses B. McIntyre, his wife Clara, and son Maurice were on the third floor. Across from them was the Hughes family. Mr. Hughes, a cousin of poet-novelist Langston Hughes, maintained a publishing firm in the basement of the building. He had about six or seven children. The oldest, Edward, contracted polio and died. The rest of us were scared to death that we might catch it, but none of us did.

Above us on the second floor was Mr. and Mrs. George Van Peebles, who owned the tailor and pressing shop in the basement. Their two sons, Edwin G. and Melvin, future composer and musician Maurice McIntyre, and our cousin Ethan, were everyday playmates for Frank and me. Melvin would make his mark on American culture by creating and starring in the film *Sweet Sweetback's Baadasssss Song*, which helped usher in Black-centric filmmaking. His son Mario continues that tradition.

Our group of runnin' buddies had many adventures in Washington Park, a block and a half away from our building, which we endlessly explored. The 380-acre park, designed by Frederick Law Olmstead (of Central Park fame), stretched from South Parkway on the west side to Cottage Grove on the east. It ran from 51st Street south to 60th Street. On the east boundary was a botanical garden and maintenance facility. Across Cottage Grove ran the Midway, a wide boulevard with a grass-covered sunken lawn that wound all the way to Stoney Island Avenue. The road cut through the entire campus of the University of Chicago, Jackson Park, and up to the lakefront and the beaches.

In the winter, one or two blocks of the park were flooded for ice skating or pick-up hockey games. Always on Thanksgiving and before family dinner, we gathered for our annual "Turkey Bowl" tackle football game. The park was our refuge for sports, picnics, parades, and civic celebrations like Bud Billikens Day (the second largest parade in the U.S. celebrating youth, education, and African American life) and Easter Sunday. There was a public swimming pool, tennis courts that "evolved" into basketball courts, and a lagoon with a boat house for fishing or rowing.

We played in sandlot football leagues. The Chicago American Giants of the Negro Baseball League ran a summer baseball camp for us. This was, of course, before Jackie Robinson broke the color barrier. There were few Black players in professional football but none in baseball or basketball yet. You can see why people of my generation cried when Barack Obama became the 44th President of the United States. As Black kids, our idols were entertainers, the few professional athletes who managed to break through, like Jack Johnson, Joe Lewis, or "Sugar Ray" Robinson and the doctors, lawyers, and educators from our neighborhoods. The adults in our families probably had a lot more power and influence over our lives than we as adults now have over the next generation. We certainly didn't have as many sources of information or devices to connect us to information.

However, our whole family listened to the radio every evening. In addition, my parents had a terrific record collection and a Victrola, a record player for the RCA Victor Company, to support their growing media industry. Some were powered by electricity; others had a windup, manual, spring-driven mechanism. On days when we couldn't play outside, we put on a record, like Fats Waller. Everybody in the room knew the whole thing by heart. We heard our parents partying to these records every weekend (and in the Smith household, every day). We chose parts until everyone had one.

"Who's gonna be Fats?"

"I'll be the tenor player; he's got a solo in the second chorus!"

"I'm the bass player this time!"

Then we started the record. This was pre-Karaoke in the late 1930s and early '40s, and we had the whole record covered! If someone missed a cue, they heard about it all day.

Our repertoire included Ellington's *Black Brown and Beige*, a symphonic work that Duke called "a parallel to the history of the Negro in America." We knew every note. Ditto for Louis Jordan and the Tympani Five. We learned everything they put out. We could do The Orioles with Sonny Til and a few other vocal groups, but just about anything that caught our fancy was something we learned.

To put our fascination with this music in perspective, when James Moody's "Mood for Love" came out with lyrics by Eddie Jefferson, not just us, but the whole neighborhood knew the arrangement. For years afterward, I walked down the street, and someone's radio was playing it. All the passers-by chimed in, just like in church. Now that's culture. That's what coming up on the South Side did for you.

There were few times in my life when I found a group of people who took the time to work out an idea just to develop it for the sake of experimentation. These cats spoiled me for life. And we were just doing it for fun then. These informal sessions went on for several years. Eventually, commitments to school and a growing interest in social affairs separated us from that kind of camaraderie.

For first grade, I attended A.O. Sexton Grade School in the neighborhood where my Uncle Neal and his family lived. Although the Carter School was right down the block, Moms didn't like the environment. We used Uncle Neal's address to justify my going to Sexton. We always made adjustments like that. If it meant staying with grandparents or cousins during the week or whatever, it was cool. We were all so close that it never made any difference. In fact, it made us all stronger. The bonds definitely deepened among us all.

My best friend in that class was Henry Dungee, who moved to the brand-new Ida B. Wells Public Housing Development, which stretched from 33rd to 35th Streets north to south and from South Parkway to Cottage Grove Avenue west to east.

My most vivid memory of first grade was of a girl in my class named Biola Johnson. Our teacher was strict and rather mean. Every day Biola came in late because she had to help her younger siblings, and every day the teacher whipped

Biola in front of the class. I hated that. I never got over it. I vowed that if I ever became a teacher, I would never treat a human being that way. I hope I have kept my promise over these many decades.

# CHAPTER 5

## *Maywood, Chickens & My First Gigs*

At the start of second grade, everything changed. Frank and I moved in with Ma and Dad so we could transfer to Washington Grade School in Maywood. That's where Moms and her relatives had attended school. It was the only mostly Black school in the mostly white District 89. My mother was displeased by recent events around A.O. Sexton, so my brother started in the first grade at Washington while I attended second grade. Two days later, Frank skipped first grade since he already knew how to read, write, and count. Transferred to my classroom, we remained classmates all the way through to the end of high school.

To put this move in context, nobody liked the schools in Chicago in the South Side for the same reasons that a lot of people are taking their kids out to the suburbs these days. But in our case, there was an even more pressing reason. Our grandparents needed some help, and they wouldn't accept any money. So Dad and Ma talked our parents into letting Frank and me stay there, go to school during the week, and come back to the South Side on the weekends.

It was on Dad's radio that I was first exposed to bebop. I was nine years old. Billy Eckstine was in Chicago when he formed that famous bebop big band left over from the group Earl "Fatha" Hines ran. That's the band Dizzy Gillespie took over from Mr. B; he gave Diz the arrangements and his best wishes. The rest is history. When I returned to the South Side as a teenager, I came to know most of the musicians as friends of my father and uncles.

Maywood was more semi-country than a suburb. We used to call it Plum Nelly: Plum out to the city and Nelly end to the country. Its unpaved streets, tall trees, and wide-open spaces cut quite a contrast to Chicago. Yes, the whole deal was bucolic, but it presented new personal challenges for me. To put it bluntly, my grandparents and my parents were urban people with country roots, but I'm urban-born and urban-rooted all the way.

I grew to fear the four words Ma yelled from the kitchen window.

"Bring me a chicken."

That meant a dead chicken.

One that I was supposed to kill.

Ma's method was to walk slowly into the middle of the flock of chickens in the backyard and scatter a few grains of chicken feed around. Then she'd snatch one by the throat and start swinging it around in a furious circle until the head was in her hand and the chicken was walking around with its head torn off.

But I was too chicken to do that shit! I wasn't mean enough.

I got the hatchet, chopped its head off, and fought to manage it. Well, that wasn't good enough. Dad and Ma, country-rooted, thought that when the chicken saw the hatchet, it would tense up. That meant that the meat would be tough when it got cooked. I wasn't tough enough to deliver tender chicken.

As for the other kids in this new neighborhood, Frank and I had to fight our way back to our grandparents' house every day after school until they learned we were "Mr. Derrick's grandkids."

We began to make friends that have lasted for a lifetime.

There were many cousins from my mother's side, too. The Hathaways were one branch; Mable was the oldest of Walter and Queenella (Watson) Hathaways' children. Lucille married one of the Singleton brothers from Broadview. They were the only Black family that lived in Broadview, just south of Maywood, at that time. Their son, Ken, became a famous professional baseball player and is now a TV sports journalist. Then there was Gwendolyn, Bernice, Watson, and Betty, the youngest. Gerald and Tommy Sampson, our Aunt Ruth's children, were born the same year and month as Frank and me—May and June.

We made it through the same grade school and high school that most of our parents had attended. Betty met and married Grady Rivers in high school. Their son, Glen "Doc" Rivers, is a professional NBA coach. Another cousin, Richard Smith, lived with his grandparents on 14th Street. We lived on 13th Street. The Hathaways were on 12th, almost across from Washington school, where most Black kids and several families of white kids attended.

All day, we roamed the nearby Catherine Chevalier Forest Preserve. The Des Plaines River ran through the preserve, providing us with countless adventures. Like Washington Park, the river delivered an occasional tragedy, usually in winter, when someone fell in while trying to cross the ice.

To illustrate how deep in the boonies we were, we biked for miles out to the Army Airport, which eventually became O'Hare International. Although we had no bicycle gears or racing tires, we rode all day.

Now here's where fate gets tricky. During the Second World War, the train of thought of American military leaders was that Black men weren't courageous enough to go into serious battle with the "enemy." Could they have thought that we might turn against our white countrymen? So all the Black recruits from Maywood were sent out as orderlies, cooks, and other non-combat details. A battalion of soldiers containing all the white enlistees from Maywood was sent to the Pacific, where Japanese forces wiped them out in an infamous battle and death march. A Hollywood movie, *Bataan*, starring John Wayne, made years later, told that story.

The Black soldiers came back, and the town turned Black within one generation.

During my grade school years in Maywood, I had my first job playing drums with my father's band. Included on the bandstand that night was a young baritone sax player named Laurdine Patrick, whom everyone called Pat. He went on to play with composer-pianist-bandleader Sun Ra, touring and traveling the world. We ended up teaching together on the faculty of SUNY/Old Westbury for many years. His son, Deval Patrick, would become the governor of Massachusetts from 2007 to 2015.

With the family band, we covered all the standard tunes: Ellington, Basie, and Cole Porter. Everything that was popular, from New Orleans to Fletcher Henderson, and the radio music in the 1930s and '40s. We played primarily swing music, and I learned the repertoire and the lyrics to all the songs. I had standard arrangements and all this stuff in my memory before starting college.

I loved playing with Pops and my cousins, but I still had a lot to learn about not being a knucklehead. For example, there was a place on Wabash Avenue called Bacon's Casino, a Quonset hut structure—that is, a long tent with a curved roof and flat sides. All the cats in town or passing through—in those years, it might be Roy Eldridge or Coleman Hawkins—made that a jam session on Sunday after church. Naturally, the Smith clan was usually in full attendance. Naïve and arrogant, I tried to sit in once on bass, playing by ear Charlie Parker's lively "Cherokee" of all things. I was cool until we got to the bridge.

Afterward, my fingers were burned up! That's the know-it-all path I badly needed to outgrow.

One of the first things that helped me was getting into the District 89 School Band. I was the only Black musician in the band at that time, although Willie Dixon, a saxophonist who also became a professional, had preceded me as a barrier breaker. Twice a week, I was excused from Washington to go to another school in the district to rehearse. I loved it. This new context gave me a better understanding of my skill and how to improve it.

It was the first of many musical borders I would cross. As a result of this crucial band experience, I was immediately accepted into the Proviso Township High School Concert Band, where I attended high school.

# CHAPTER 6

## *Wagner, Teen Blues & Musician or Architect*

District 89 School Band proved a quantum leap in my musical exposure. I played with the most talented students my age in the district. Our musical teacher and director, J. Irving Talmadge, was a huge fan of German composer Richard Wagner. I learned to play almost everything Wagner wrote, from the "Ring of the Nebilungen" to "Taunhauser Overture." My musical vocabulary expanded. I was exposed to the timpani for the first time and had the chance to learn the basics of the instrument.

I also played bass drums in the Proviso Township High School Marching Band. Although I abhorred all the marching, I loved performing at the football games.

Nevertheless, after my freshman year at Proviso, I grew away from music as my primary focus for the first and only time in my life. I stopped taking weekly lessons from my most significant teacher at the time, Oliver S. Coleman. The commute from Maywood, my expanding social life, and my athletic training (I joined the track team and started running long-distance races the year before) all played a part.

In addition, I was a teenager contemplating my future career. I loved music and knew that I would always play it. But I saw firsthand that Chicago was a tough town to make a living exclusively by performing. Pops and many talented relatives moved on to other employment when gigs were slow. One of my cousins, James Smith, whom we all called Sonny, illustrated the dilemma Black musicians faced in the Windy City. An electrical engineer by day, Sonny played jazz guitar by night. When he switched to electric bass, he worked steadily with Chester Burnett (Howlin' Wolf) for several years but kept his day job. Wolf was a giant of Chicago blues and one of its greatest pioneers, but even a steady gig with him did not ensure a livelihood.

I began to develop a more serious interest in architecture. I had so much encouragement to explore this field of study, thanks to my friend Joe Black, an art teacher at Proviso High School, and especially Pops, who made me aware of Frank Lloyd Wright and the Bauhaus gang with their glass and steel buildings in downtown Chicago. My folks bought me a Kodak Brownie camera, which gave me a chance to photograph these architectural wonders.

Only two things kept me connected with music at this time. One was the opportunity to perform in Washington Park with Captain Walter Henry Dyett and his summer concert band, which was as famous for producing future professional musicians as the present-day universities that feed the NFL and the NBA. Countless numbers of Captain Dyett's students wound up in New York; many became famous recording artists.

The other music connection was the chance to hear the legendary "High Jinks" concert that the students at DuSable High School put on every year. My older cousin Edwin Earl Smith, whom we all called Eddie, played in the sax section along with Johnny Griffin, who was at the start of a great career in jazz.

As for our home life, after our second year at Proviso, Ma died. Rather than be a burden to our grandfather, Frank and I moved back to 58th Street and commuted to Maywood on the Bluebird bus every morning.

Being back on the South Side again had many advantages, both social and musical, for us two high school kids. In the mid-to-late 1940s, the big theaters in the Loop offered a movie and a live stage show featuring groups like Benny Goodman's band or Tommy Dorsey's band with vocalists. The Regal Theater on the South Side featured Duke Ellington, Count Basie, Lionel Hampton, Buddy Johnson, and Cab Calloway. Next to the Regal was the Savoy Ballroom, which hosted big affairs with live music and social dancing. It also had a roller-skating rink, which was immensely popular.

Although we each had our own tastes and preferences, all music had merit in our household. My folks had a range of records they played when friends dropped in. Pops introduced me to all the 19th-century Romantic composers, especially the French and Russian. I knew all this music before I went to college to study it because he listened to it all the time. He was also open to the new. I remember being at a dance where Charlie Parker was in the band. Our parents were there as chaperones but also as fans. Digging it as much as we did, they could relax because no kid would play the fool in front of their family and neighbors.

Many people of his swing jazz generation dismissed the beboppers for being anti-jazz and destroying the music, but if you listened closely, they weren't lacking in technical proficiency. They just heard a different set of changes that the older musicians weren't accustomed to. Over and over, I've seen something genius and original get resisted before finally becoming accepted. Some bop-based musicians resisted what John Coltrane and Ornette Coleman were doing. I felt the same way toward hip-hop, for instance. But I realized where that came from. I gave it a little more time and saw how it developed.

In the early 1950s several jazz clubs showcased live music. The Kit Cat Club had Ahmad Jamal's trio (until they moved over to the lounge at the Pershing Hotel). We heard Dizzy Gillespie, Miles Davis, John Coltrane, Max Roach and Clifford Brown, Art Blakey, and Horace Silver with the early Jazz

Messengers featuring Doug Watkins on bass, Hank Mobley on tenor, and Donald Byrd on trumpet. We also heard local jazz talent like Gene Ammons as well as blues and R&B artists performing around the city.

On our way to church on Sundays, Frank and I stopped at Mr. Blount's stand to get our shoes shined. A relative of Sun Ra (Herman Poole Blount), Mr. Blount told us that he was so poor as a child that he'd put shoe polish on his ankles to hide the fact that he had no socks. At Sunday school, we met our friends and sat through the session. But as church started, we stepped out and went to the Met Music Shop, which sold all the latest releases from Nat King Cole, Erroll Garner, and the be-boppers. Back then, you took a record into a booth and listened before deciding to buy it. Two or three of us crowded into the booth, but one of us played sentry, keeping an eye peeled for folks coming out of church.

I could not imagine a city any more active and vibrant than this, especially on weekends. And it wasn't just music. For example, the local YMCA sponsored a group of us high school students. Called the "Hi Y," several of us joined this integrated group. We shared our cultural heritage. One month we met at a Jewish student's house. The next time, we'd gather at an Italian student's home. Jacobus Richardson, Jr., hosted the meeting in our part of town. Of course, we had ham, fried chicken, collard greens, and cornbread. We enjoyed the experience and learned something new with each visit and meal. Little did I realize it then, but these experiences of crossing cultural and social borders in my formative years were building my confidence, stimulating my curiosity, and opening me up as a human being.

On Saturdays, some of us from the Church of the Good Shepherd, plus a few other cousins and friends, formed a discussion club that met at our neighborhood YMCA. Called the Omicrons, in imitation of the Greek fraternal organizations on college campuses, we continued to meet into adulthood. To this day, we are still in frequent contact with each other, but now we talk about our grandchildren rather than ourselves.

During the year, we trekked over to the Museum of Science and Industry. I especially liked the informational exhibits: a miniature coal mine, steel mill, railroad, and assorted architectural wonders.

Although we were segregated residentially, there was rarely any racial conflict. Even the "bad boys" at Washington School were generally cooled out by the time they got to Proviso Township High School, which had more than a thousand freshmen coming in each year from the feeder schools in District 89. Of the 765 students in our graduating class of 1952, 18 were Black; nine of us went on to college.

The day after my graduation, I started working at the post office and stayed throughout the summer. Then my brother and I enrolled in the University of Illinois at Urbana-Champaign. We were two of the 300 Black students in a population of 20,000. We were ready.

# CHAPTER 7

## *Alpha House, Paul Price & the Percussion Ensemble*

My life was now divided between Champaign and the South Side. I rarely went back to Maywood except to visit my relatives on occasion. Frank and I didn't know when we left for college that we were leaving 58th Street forever. When we returned for Thanksgiving break, the family had relocated to 4428 ½ South Drexel Boulevard.

A whole lot of changes happened—and fast. Frank and I moved into the Alpha Phi Alpha Fraternity House, where I spent the next five academic years. We lived in the town of Champaign, where we discovered that Moms was related to the mother of our frat brother, Welbourne Bowles. His brother, Quinton Bowles, studied percussion with me in the school's music department. Quinton Bowles's future wife, Alfreda, was a piano major from the west side of Chicago.

The Bowles were a big extended family and a delightful trove of relatives. So were the Ridgewaters. These friends and relatives were good, even necessary, to know. The whole five years that I was there, there was no hotel in Champaign or Urbana that would accommodate my parents when they came down for a visit or graduation and stayed overnight. So, they stayed with relatives and friends.

Frank and I shared a room at the top of the Alpha House; it was big enough for three, so our older cousin Eddie joined us. He played clarinet in the marching band and the First Regimental band of the U of I and majored in music education. The following May, he received his undergraduate degree, entered the seminary, and became an Episcopal minister; he is now a retired canon of the church. Eddie is the middle brother. His elder brother, Dr. Neal Dow, Jr., earned his Ph.D. in chemical engineering. A brilliant scientist, he worked as a vice president at US Steel. Eddie's younger brother, Ethan Allen, was a year younger than Frank. Eddie's brothers were brilliant musicians. They could sing, play piano by ear, and discuss the finer aesthetics of music and styles with any of my professional friends. But Eddie took it further. His influence on me was profound. He, Pops, and Dad were my real role models. It wasn't just their acumen or level of engagement. Their entire approach to life could be summed up in one phrase: compassion to all. And that's what came through their being and their music.

That's what I was after as well. But I was now enrolled (somewhat uncertainly) in the School of Fine Arts, Architecture. Frank was in the School of Visual Arts, and it was clear he was in the right place, especially after we got our class schedules. I knew he would do well with his courses; I wasn't as convinced about my courses. Eddie and I walked over to the band headquarters and qualified for the First Regimental band and the Marchin' Illini, the university's marching band, which paid each of us fifty dollars per semester.

I next met my percussion teacher, Professor Paul William Price, another major influence who would change my life. Born in Massachusetts, he had studied the developments in composition from the Romantic tradition to the most contemporary, including Karlheinz Stockhausen, Gunther Schuller, and Darius Milhaud. These composers helped break us out of that rigid classical music box.

I signed up for Professor Price's percussion lessons, starting with marimba and snare drum. He was the most meticulously disciplined teacher I have ever studied with. He made me realize that every note I played was important. Every triangle beat, bass drum roll, or vibraphone chord should be executed precisely and within the composer's specifications. He showed me how to pull the desired sound out of the instrument.

With this heaven-sent percussion instructor, I learned European classical music's nuances. I also played melodically (marimba) after years on the (non-melodic) drum kit. In addition, Professor Price invited me to join the music department's percussion ensemble, one of the first in any university.

Like so many of the remarkable things that had already happened to me—playing with my father and cousins, grade school and high school concerts and marching bands, and Captain Dyett's summer concert band—Professor Price's percussion ensemble was a right place/right time and right skills/right fit kind of deal. Photographer Ansel Adams once said, "Chance favors the well-prepared," and I had a sense that as long as I kept woodshedding and growing as a musician, unique opportunities like this might appear. It was a level of serendipity that felt providential and proved a turning point in my musical education.

It was also my first taste of controversy. Professor Price's percussion ensemble was so ultra-modern and pioneering that some proponents of the "classical tradition" saw it as a threat to their legitimacy. They tried to denigrate it as less challenging than 17th-century music from Vienna. Of course, by the mid-20th century, it was too late to turn back. The genie was out of the bottle. I am not even discussing improvisation yet, even though 17th-century concerto forms required that the soloist improvise a cadenza of their creativity. I'm talking about contemporary composers like John Cage, who required instrumentalists to do things they hadn't heard or tried before. The percussion ensemble performed *Ionisation For Thirteen Percussionists* by Edgar Varèse, *Tres Ritmos* by Carlos Roldan, Lou Harrison's *Canticle #3*, and works by Cage—all demanding but fascinating scores.

To his credit, Professor Paul Price was an enterprising director. He arranged tours for us to play at other colleges and high schools. We went on the road almost every semester for a week or ten days. Invariably, we found out where the jazz clubs and the jam sessions were. I remember seeing Kenny Burrell's quartet with Yusef Lateef and Paul Chambers in Detroit. But on these tours, we didn't associate with the students in these music departments all that much. There was much rivalry, which often raised its head when we least expected it. One would think young people studying our classical tradition would have an interest in pioneers who crossed musical borders, but what we played was too new or too much for some.

Because we employed a variety of percussion instruments from various cultures, we were accused of being, among other things, too African. In this crowd, that was bad news. The underlying mistaken certainty prevalent in that era was that African drums were so primitive that they required no study and could be played by any western-trained musician. Another discrepancy for the more rectilinear was that we performed scores with improvisational passages, making it not "classical enough."

To put this exclusionary point of view in context, some falsely (automatically) assumed that musicians who could improvise well lacked sight reading skills. As for a tradition of improvisation like jazz, the conservatory dismissed it back then as a distraction, a novelty, an insignificant fad. The music was deemed inferior, something without value, sophistication, and grace. Forget Charlie Parker playing for Igor Stravinsky! Forget those French composers who soaked up jazz harmonies!

Such a snobby point of view resulted from fear, as if their sense of cultural superiority was being challenged. Ironically, theirs was a rejection of world music, not just of Africa but of Asia, the Middle East, and of Native peoples everywhere. My disagreement with this thinking was so profound that I felt it in my bones. But in this dismissive environment, I felt no need to mention my experiences playing popular contemporary music and the joy and satisfaction it brought me.

I had never encountered a percussion ensemble before. And I hadn't even gotten into African percussion music at that point. Professor Price had a warrior spirit and fought the battle for legitimacy, but it was a trial by fire. He was ambitious and developed this incredible percussion ensemble, yet everybody accused him of being beneath classical music and playing the bongo drums down in Bongo Bongo land. That's how the U of I program got stereotyped among the other big schools. He kept bringing in new people with progressive ideas and incurred the animosity of less ambitious faculty members. Eventually, he moved to the Big Apple and joined the Manhattan School of Music faculty.

Observing the difficulties Professor Price went through made me realize that music education needed people like him as well as me. I loved music, and I liked students who loved to learn. Too many music teachers I encountered did not. I rebelled against what I saw as an abuse of authority. Instructors used their knowledge to intimidate students and dictate personal tastes rather than inspire and inquire about what makes music tasteful.

Professor Price's extracurricular tours were essential to a complete education, and one event stands out as a reminder that this binary approach to music—the classical tradition was art and the popular music was not—was overdue for revision. On one trip to Pittsburgh, we wound up at the Black Musicians' Union. Like Chicago, their unions hadn't integrated yet, but they had a jam session. The whole University of Illinois percussion ensemble came to hang out. The guy running the session was a small, neatly dressed drummer named Cecil Brooks. His son is a drummer in New Jersey and runs a club that presents live music. At any rate, none of us were confident enough to ask to sit in, but we learned more from just listening. These folks were seasoned professionals, much like my relatives and their associates, and what they played left no doubt about their chops, artistry, or dedication to the music.

Although I loved these musical encounters, hellhounds were on my trail. My grades in non-music courses plummeted. One glaring example was my freehand rendering; it was not on par with my peers. Some of them looked like they were using a camera. In my overconfident style, I thought I could draw better than Frank. To put it bluntly, drawing classes whipped my ass. I just barely got by with a D while I got all A grades in my music classes.

I felt torn apart by conflicting desires. As a teenager developing my skills on the drums, I often overheard my father's associates telling him to send me to the Big Apple. As I got older and better, these folks got bolder and more direct.

"Boy," they told me point blank, "get yourself outta here and go to New York." Perhaps they recognized that I had the talent to succeed but suspected I might not get the chance to use that talent to my fullest advantage in Chicago. In high school, I had dismissed music as a career pursuit, but here I was in college and not making it in architecture. It was time for a few changes.

I had to find the courage to make them.

# CHAPTER 8

## *Timpani, Ike's Inauguration & the Marchin' Illini*

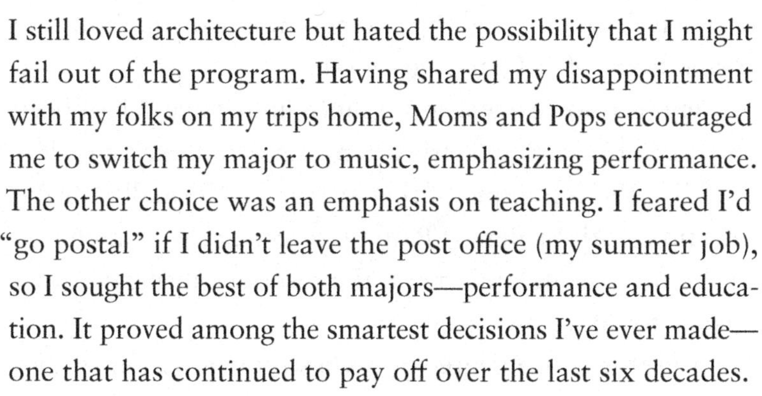

I still loved architecture but hated the possibility that I might fail out of the program. Having shared my disappointment with my folks on my trips home, Moms and Pops encouraged me to switch my major to music, emphasizing performance. The other choice was an emphasis on teaching. I feared I'd "go postal" if I didn't leave the post office (my summer job), so I sought the best of both majors—performance and education. It proved among the smartest decisions I've ever made—one that has continued to pay off over the last six decades.

At the time, the decision was agonizing. There were no more than a half dozen Black students who were majors in the U of I music department, and most were in education, not performance. As my string teacher advised me, "Now, Smith, you'd better take these music education classes more seriously because you know there is no place in professional music for a Negro!"

That was the low ceiling that my high-flying ambitions crashed up against. Langston Hughes' poem came to mind. In the first line, he asked, "What happens to a dream deferred?"

He answered it in the last line: "Or does it explode?"

Fortunately, my dream got a lot more realistic by my freshman spring semester. I dropped art and architecture courses. I learned a great deal in my music classes, both theory and performance. I also played in four different musical groups on campus: the Marchin' Illini, the First Regimental band, the symphony orchestra, and the percussion ensemble. I ran on the freshman track team and was a newly initiated member of Tau Chapter of Alpha Phi Alpha fraternity. It may have been a rough first semester, but throughout the spring term, I felt I had it goin' on.

My second year was even more immersive. I had been fascinated by timpani (kettle drums) since grade school. Now I studied the technique of this instrument formally for the first time with Professor Paul Price. Since I was in charge of the percussion equipment, the responsibility gave me a chance for extra practice.

A performance degree in orchestral percussion studies focused on three instruments: snare drum, marimba (I was now in my second semester in both), and timpani. In addition, some scores in symphonic music may have the percussionist playing xylophone, vibraphone, glockenspiel, concert bass drum, concert toms, triangle, castanets, tambourine, or cymbals. I grew proficient at playing these instruments as well.

This pioneering adventure into performing classical music in the percussion chair was thrilling. I had the advantage of first learning saxophone, so working with melodies, chords, tones, and pitches via mallets felt natural. The only real challenge in my undergraduate years was my patience regarding the university's narrow point of view, culturally speaking. The history of Western civilization that they taught (especially about all things Black) was antithetical to the information passed down from my family. Having "learned" since high school about how insignificant my people allegedly were, the whole subject turned me off. The result was that I had to take this course a second time to graduate.

The other bump in the road was music theory. The terminology was not what I was used to hearing from my family and the musicians who hung out with us. It took me at least a year to figure out how to apply the terms to what I already knew.

I flunked swimming, not because I couldn't swim but because the class was held at eight o'clock in the morning. The water was freezing cold, the chlorine irritated my eyes, and I missed too many classes. I had to take that over again, as well, but I found a more suitable hour and a pair of goggles.

I cannot emphasize enough how much the performance side of my education developed my skill set. Besides touring with the percussion ensemble, we left school with the marching band, riding together on a bus to the away football games to support the team. The Marchin' Illini was among the best marching bands in the nation. We played Dwight Eisenhower's presidential inauguration in January 1953 in Washington, D.C. I would love to say how proud I felt to march in the parade, but it was an exercise in extreme personal restraint.

For context, segregation was the law of the land, and the (all white) marching band directly behind us was from the University of Mississippi. Being Black in a racially integrated marching band from up North was one thing, but we were south of the Mason-Dixon line. What put my game in check was that I, the last member of the entire band, stood in a wagon playing two timpani while a white member hauled me and my gear along Pennsylvania Avenue.

The indignity of a Black musician carted around by a white man was too much for the Ole Miss Marching Band. However, they waited until after we passed the presidential platform before threatening my life, slandering my mother, and taunting my family. Though I heard every possible slur imaginable and its variation, I was cool. But just barely. It was the first time I was glad we kept marching.

As for Champaign and Urbana, there was a jazz scene in both towns. On campus, they had an organization called "Jazz U Like It" which featured some students and local musicians. The university had special events presented throughout the school year. Symphonic orchestras from Europe and famous personalities from all over performed for the students and faculty.

We also had jazz specials that featured Art Tatum, Charlie Parker, Dizzy Gillespie, Thelonius Monk, Coleman Hawkins, and a young Miles Davis. Duke Ellington's band played for a school dance, and his drummer, Dave Black, used two bass drums. It was the first time I had seen that! Stan Kenton featuring the Four Freshmen, a singing group, played for another dance. Every year, James Moody came to Danville to play a gig in a club there with an eight-piece ensemble of five horns and a rhythm section. We got a ride over there each time they came. The musical arrangements were so modern.

The multiple-performance schedule kept me busy, but I found ways of making some side money. I set up the percussion equipment for all orchestra rehearsals, which paid me a small stipend of a hundred dollars, which coincidentally was the tuition price per semester. My gig in food service at the dormitory cafeteria also brought in some coin, and I got to eat for free. I bartended with a friend who developed a small business serving social affairs. We got a fee and a share of the tips, which was often larger than the fee.

Although necessary and in their own way valuable, these mundane activities were contrasted by the unearthly music of composers whose work we were learning, rehearsing, and performing: Varèse, Cage, Schuller, Charles Wourinen, and so many other unique voices. Schuller came as a guest to the U of I as a composer; he wasn't even interested in "jazz" at that time. He was just trying to break out of the box of classical music and get into what he called the third stream. I soaked up all of these influences. Our faculty had Ben Johnson. He was my favorite music theory teacher; he was deeply into the music, and so was just about everyone in the program.

Although I still loved jazz, I was fully immersed in classical music, its composition, arrangement, and execution in both its traditional and avant-garde wings.

# CHAPTER 9

## *John Cage, the Water Gong & the Tanglewood Blues*

I had no idea of the wild ride I was about to catch in the fall of 1955.

I had completed my junior year recital and began to prepare the material for my senior recital. I enjoyed playing in Professor Price's percussion ensemble. He especially loved the work of John Cage, and he had enough juice to get the music department to sponsor regular visits by Cage to the U of I.

By the mid-Fifties, John Cage had already achieved world-wide recognition as an innovative and highly original composer. I could see why Professor Price was fascinated. Cage sought new approaches to harmony and making music using sound, silence, chance, improvisation, and experimentation.

Instead of a fully notated music score, Cage gave a one-sentence instruction to the performer. For example, his (in)famous and controversial composition "4'33," he insisted on the absence of any sound made by the performer for four minutes and thirty-three seconds. The focus was on the sounds of the environment heard by the audience. The empty (note-free) composition was a record (or report or resonance) of the moment's audio scape. Cage was cagey like a Zen master.

Among other places, he had been teaching at Black Mountain, an experimental college in North Carolina that was home to Abstract Expressionist painters, Projective Verse, New York School poets, and modern dance students. It was where Cage created *Theatre Piece #1*, the first "happening," a multi-layered multimedia performance that would become a Sixties template in many avant-garde circles. He also began writing musical scores to the choreography of his domestic partner Merce Cunningham and his dance company.

I remember one of the first encounters we had. He told us that we could turn the musical score upside down and play it that way. We were free to do whatever we wanted with it. He sat and enjoyed the effects of it. And I realized that such an approach takes some real trust on his part. But it always seemed to work. It even got to the point where he wrote a piece purposefully to antagonize the audience and then include the audience's reactions as part of the composition like, "I can't stand to hear this shit!" I came to see that hatred and love are two powerful but kindred emotions that can be intertwined to produce something new.

Besides pioneering the use of prepared piano (altering its sound by placing objects on its strings or hammers), Cage also had a few of his own instruments. For one of his compositions, he taught our percussion ensemble how to play a water gong. He had us fill a bathtub with water, strike the hand-held gong with a mallet, let it vibrate awhile, and then put it underwater quickly so the sound ends with a whoop.

When we performed, I got the call to play the water gong. I knew this particular score well, and just before my cue I found a sight line to Cage. I watched his face as the water gong made an unusually abrupt and dramatic whoop. The man almost fell out of his chair. To call his expression orgasmic was an understatement. His face was a combination of delight, surprise, joy, and discovery.

This percussion effect came out better than he expected—that's what his look conveyed. It was the first time I had sought out a composer's reaction during a recital, but I was so knocked out to see Cage enraptured like that. It prompted me to seek out a composer's reaction when performing their music.

John Cage liked what we did with his compositions so much that he brought the entire percussion ensemble to New York City to make Concert Percussion for Orchestra. It included five Cage pieces and works by Amadeo Roldan, Roy Harrison, Henry Cowell (Cage's teacher) and William Russell. I played timbales and percussion. Cage and Professor Price conducted.

It was my first recording, and it felt like a most auspicious beginning (I would go on to play on over three thousand recording sessions). I played my best with great musicians and excellent scores. I did not know it at the time, but working with a spiritual seeker and musical pioneer like John Cage prepared me for composers like Harry Partch, Charles Mingus, and Gil Evans.

As the spring semester of 1956 ended, I had yet to be invited to the Tanglewood Summer Music Camp.

After inquiring, Professor Price said he thought I wasn't interested. The year before, I passed on a chance to attend the Aspen Summer Music Camp in Colorado. I had been intent on working at the post office that summer to pay for the university tuition for Frank and me. But this year, I had already earned the money we needed. I got up my nerve and told Professor Price that I was very interested in attending Tanglewood.

All it took was his recommendation. Tanglewood awarded me a scholarship for the summer session.

Off to the Berkshire Mountains to play classical symphonic music for six weeks, I wondered how isolated we would be. I reassured myself that the music department of the University of Illinois and the city of Chicago were well represented. There were singers Herb Scott Gibson and Harold Johnson, Dave Moore and Ben Patterson, bassists, violinists Sanford Allen and Marie Hence, sopranos Annabelle Bernard and Shirley Verrett Carter, and choral conductor

Leroy Thompson. When Harold Johnson told me that The Chicago Defender was coming up to take a colored picture, I dressed for technicolor. When only the Black musicians showed up for the photo shoot, I caught on.

The other thing that put any sense of isolation to rest was that we played this beautiful music daily. It was a serious classical music hang and a real generational exchange of teaching and learning. Even former student Leonard Bernstein came up and conducted us one day. The old timpani master, Roman Szulc, was in his retirement year, so I benefited from his coaching. He showed me how to extract a beautiful sound from the instrument, how to get full leverage from your mallet, exactly where on the head to strike for a certain texture or sound, the proper speed or roll pulsation, and many other tips.

The incoming young gun Everett "Vic" Firth was often there so I could observe and compare the two. The old man, Szulc, was warm, soft, and tender. Vic, on the other hand, was a Juilliard student with that hard and fast New York attitude, but I learned a lot from him professionally. In addition, the first percussionist of the Boston Symphony Orchestra, Harold Farberman, and I became good friends. I studied snare drum technique with him. I use his information to this day for my students.

Playing percussion to great works all day and sleeping outdoors in a tent pitched beside a small mountain lake, I felt completely ensconced in beauty. On certain days, after hearing or performing in a great orchestral work, I considered that I might stop playing jazz altogether. Seduced by the whole classical music world, the craftmanship and camaraderie of the players, and the blending of so many symphonic parts into a single sound, I saw myself playing Dvořák and Sibelius and those beautiful timpani parts for the length of my life.

Then one day, I got in the car to get a haircut. Driving out of the campus area, I turned on the radio and heard the blues. I didn't even know I liked the blues that much until right then. It hit me so hard! I had internalized the power of that sound and its soul force. I had disrespected the simplicity of the form and hadn't yet heard all the forms.

I had a bad case of the Tanglewood blues. I felt homesick. I realized how much I missed my family, how interconnected my family was, this blues music, and where I was from. When I returned to Chicago, I started hanging out at all the old blues clubs and learning a lot more. But it took me a few years around a few more scenes before the multiple musical genres I was studying and playing as a drummer and percussionist started mixing, mating, and mutating.

All the old boundaries were about to break. Crossing a few borders as a musician only made me more in demand for what was ahead. The radio was not my only reminder of my musical roots. Across the road from the Tanglewood campus was a resort hotel called Avalon. Dave Moore, who had attended the music camp the year before, knew Randy Weston played piano at the hotel bar during the week. So we often hung out.

There was also a new jazz school at Lenox, not far from Tanglewood, where drummer Max Roach taught. He came by with Donald Byrd and Sonny Rollins to listen to Randy. I had seen Max perform in 1955 at the Beehive in Chicago. The Max Roach and Clifford Brown Quintet had been called the definitive bop group of the Fifties until Clifford's fatal automobile accident earlier in the year. I could see that Max was still shocked by his co-leader's untimely death. We talked extensively that night. Hanging with one of the pioneers of jazz, not only as a drummer but also as a composer, leader, and innovator, I confided to him my intention to relocate to New York. He encouraged me to make the move and told me to look him up when I did.

Hearing the blues on the radio, talking with Max about jazz, and listening to Randy Weston play was like returning to my home years. This just complicated the decision I needed to make. I was really into the sound of symphony music, but I knew that classical opportunities were few and even fewer than few for Black musicians. Even today, there are still relatively few.

In 1949, Harlemite and timpanist extraordinaire Elayne Jones became the first person of color to play in an American orchestra pit. A world-renowned talent and an idol of mine, she retired in 1998 after fifty years of barrier-breaking. Her story sheds light on how far we have to go as Americans. To get the job with the San Francisco Symphony Orchestra, she auditioned behind a curtain, playing Stravinsky's "Sacre du Printemps" by memory. Only when the judges could not see the contestants would an impartial judgment be guaranteed.

Elayne and I played together in the New York World's Fair Orchestra in 1964 and 1965, she on the timpani and me on the drums. Her autobiography, *Little Lady with a Big Drum*, is a personal inspiration to me.

Ortiz Walton was the first Black person in my neighborhood to enter the professional, classical, musical world. My classmate from Washington School and Proviso, Ortiz also auditioned behind a curtain for a job with the Boston Symphony Orchestra. He won the competition and stayed for only six years with the BSO. He quit the orchestra and moved to San Francisco to become a sociologist but eventually returned to play the bass and pursue a career as a solo artist.

As for Tanglewood, I was surrounded by inspiring people. The level of artistry and love of music that we shared gave me the feeling that New England, at least this town, might be different from the rest of the country.

No doubt, feeling such esprit de corps, I let my guard down in public. Dave Moore, a friend from my neighborhood in Chicago, was a few years ahead of me in school at the University of Illinois. We went to a bar with Midhat Serbagi and his girlfriend Adele, who were white. Dave and I sat at a table while Midhat and Adele danced. When the record finished, Adele asked me to dance. In the middle of the song, the jukebox suddenly shut off. We looked around to figure out what had happened to the music. Then I noticed the red-faced bartender glaring at us and looking disturbed. He had just snatched the cord of the jukebox out of the wall socket.

Adele walked over to him and asked, "What's wrong?"

I didn't hear his reply; I didn't need to. The look on her tearful face told me what he said. Dave was right there beside me and moved me toward the door. Then it dawned on me that Dave and I were the only Black faces in the joint. I realized later that Dave was ready to do battle. The whole thing went over my head until we left the place. Of course, we never went back. But after that, I never forgot to look both ways.

This lesson was powerfully reinforced when I moved East two years later. I was to find that many of my Black friends in New York seemed unaware of such occurrences or were insulated from them.

Tanglewood was nevertheless an enlightening experience for me musically and professionally. Many of the people I met there went on to play a significant role in my life. Most of them ended up in the Big Apple and eventually became professional musicians.

After the six weeks in the Berkshires, I visited New York City and stayed for another week in Harlem with Moms' cousin, Hazel Coney. I got to see the original Birdland and the whole 52nd Street scene, which also set my mind to making an eventual move to the Big Apple. But there were still many events that were important to my life and my career yet to occur in both Chicago and Urbana-Champaign.

# CHAPTER 10

## *Mary, Marriage & Harry Partch*

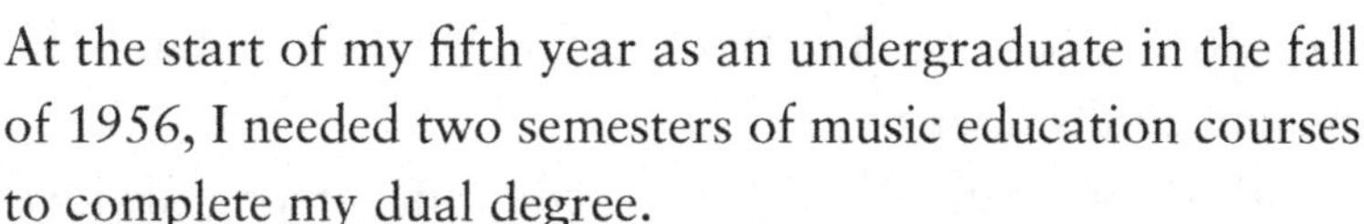

At the start of my fifth year as an undergraduate in the fall of 1956, I needed two semesters of music education courses to complete my dual degree.

Having completed all my coursework for my performance major, including my senior recital, I lightened my load even further by retiring from the Marchin' Illini and the First Regimental band. I had learned plenty by playing with the marching band in my four high school years at Proviso and my four college years at the U of I. But I was damn tired of marching. I never liked that part of the gig (and why I quit the Boy Scouts). On the other hand, I loved the power of a large group of musicians in unison. Marching was just an unnecessary "path" to playing the music.

Marching always made me think of war. I had known Black men drafted into World War Two and the Korean War, and I considered playing in a marching band as the lesser of two evils. Evil number one was getting sent off to war. I never wanted to pick up a weapon to shoot, maim, and murder human beings.

Historically speaking, as an African American, I found it difficult to trust the armed forces, especially when serving overseas. Yet returning to the States after the war often meant battling with non-Black citizens who sought to take Black veterans down a peg or two. War was a no-win situation for me. I had seen all the bombings I wanted to see just growing up in Chicago. If I needed military service, I would play music for the military band: snare drum, bass drum, kettle drum, cymbals, triangle, glockenspiel. The only killing I would do would be on those instruments. Woody Guthrie expressed it best when he wrote on his acoustic guitar, "This machine kills fascists."

If the opposite of war is love, count me among the lovestricken. I was twenty-one years old and completely unprepared for what happened to me.

I fell in love. I had known Mary since she arrived in Maywood at the tender age of eleven. She was the daughter of a doctor. Born in 1937, Mary was three years younger than me, almost to the day. She was born on May 13; I was born on May 14. To think that I had been trying to play it cool for seven years. Now she was on the University of

Illinois campus, lovelier than ever, a sophomore taking her undergraduate degree in elementary education.

A childhood crush flowered into an adult romance. We became engaged that fall. Having completed my junior and senior recital requirements, I was especially glad I had a light course load in my fifth year. Mary and I saw each other as much as possible over the next year.

Though I had quit marching band, I remained the timpanist for the University of Illinois Symphony Orchestra and Concert Band. I performed all the major literature for timpani in preparation for my transition to New York and the Manhattan School of Music, which I had applied to for my master's degree in percussion. My confidence was high, and my technique was professionally up to its mark for the percussion work I was to encounter.

Harry Partch had just begun his year-long residency at the school that semester. Except for time with Mary, I gave up a social life, as musicians do. I dedicated the two semesters to what proved to be the greatest musical and academic experience of my young life.

Working in Professor Price's percussion ensemble led to working with John Cage, whose compositions required us to use our instruments fully. But Partch was even more pioneering. He had invented a musical language to be played on his instruments. It made him the most distinctive among composers of the twentieth century, but it presented extraordinary challenges for us young music makers. Despite the difficulty, some members of our group played with Harry for many seasons. Our colleague, Dan Lee Mitchell, became musical director a few years later.

The Harry Partch Ensemble rehearsed six nights a week from six to ten. We had to learn the techniques to play his handmade instruments and non-traditional manuscripts using his original notation system with irregular rhythmic cycles. These instruments and notation systems were his life's work, which he had begun at the age of 14. He was 45 when he came to the U of I.

Musicians are accustomed to the twelve-tone system with an octave of notes, but Partch had thirty-three tones to an octave. We had to grow our ears to hear these tones. We tuned to microtonalities from his reed organ, which had a range of 66 keys that spanned one and a half octaves of the tempered (western) scale. Those of us employing conventional instruments, like strings and woodwinds, had to adapt to playing the microtonal passages by alternate fingerings and fretting positions.

The Harry Partch project included a theater piece called *The Bewitched*, which required me to learn and play the Marimba Eroica. Built in 1954, the instrument comprises four bars of Sitka spruce on top of large resonator boxes. The lowest bar sounds at 22 Hz, approximately the F below the lowest note of a piano. The audience did not actually discern the sound, but they did register the vibration of the sound in their solar plexus; they could feel it, though they could not quite hear it. This willingness to work below the human hearing level was highly instructive to me as a composer.

In addition to learning these new instruments, all of us were also cast members with scripted lines. The Alwin Nikolais Dance Company was involved, and we musicians had choreographed movements to perform as well.

At the end of the school year in May, we performed and recorded the whole production on campus for Gate Five Records. It was an extraordinary show. The company released the record in 1958 under the title *Bewitched*. That album was my second recording and as encouraging a beginning as the Cage sessions. I couldn't believe how wildly good luck had stung me. I was working with two of the most pioneering avant-garde composers of the century. These expertly made albums of their music were the proof.

The Harry Partch Ensemble then performed in St. Louis. As we celebrated afterward in the hotel lounge, someone tapped me on the shoulder. The (Black) doorman told me someone wanted to see me at the door. I was surprised, not expecting any guests, but I went to see who it was. Of course, no one was there.

As I turned to go back to the party, a voice said, "I'm sorry, you can't go back in."

I turned and saw a tall white man blocking my path.

"Why?" I asked and then volunteered, "Is it because I'm Black?"

He gave no answer.

At this point, two female classmates came out to see what was happening. We kept our heads and just moved the party upstairs to our rooms. Although we don't see this so obviously anymore (I hope not), I've never lost my apprehension about such happenings. Am I waiting to exhale? It's only been six decades.

Right after this performance, I graduated. Harry Partch was scheduled to do his next residency at Antioch College in Yellow Springs, Ohio. After the ensemble members wrapped up and carefully loaded all the precious handmade instruments, the job of driving Harry fell to me. I could not have been more pleased. On the road, we discussed his use of structured improvisation, which fascinated me; the two *Bewitched* shows were similar, but different things happened, making each performance unique.

As for the composer, he, too, was one of a kind: comical, gregarious, sophisticated, inquisitive, searching, always looking for new ways to present ideas. He talked about his relationships with other people, friends, and how they helped him survive as an American composer and not worry about making money. Thanks to wealthy patrons, he had found a way to teach his system and give concerts.

We stopped overnight at the home of one patron and friend, an executive of the Link Belt Company. The next day I dropped Harry off at the college and returned the truck to the campus in southern Illinois before going home to Chicago. When I finally got to the house, a telegram awaited me, confirming my scholarship to the Manhattan School of Music. The synchronicity stunned me. All these unrelated events in my life and education had been working together.

Harry Partch was a "classic" example. As a percussionist, I had to adapt to his unusual tones and irregular rhythmic cycles. It might be five beats against seven with different accents over thirteen full counts before you're back at the one. I went to sleep, counting it off. Thinking about rhythm in this new way had a peculiar effect on me. I could not have imagined anything more complex, yet I succeeded in learning and expressing this musical language. It did not replace the other musical languages but co-existed with them.

In tuning me to other frequencies, Partch's system helped me become more receptive to contemporary composers. Their music, however dissonant or challenging or "out," became more accessible to me. Since I had delivered what I considered the most difficult music possible, the new, the untried, and the outré intrigued me.

The Big Apple beckoned.

Before I left for New York, my last summer job was as a camp counselor for the Chicago Park District. I worked in Jackson Park at the daycare summer camp for elementary school children. Mary took summer classes in Urbana-Champaign, intending to graduate early in February and join me in New York. So, after work, I drove down to the campus over one weekend, and we eloped.

The backstory: Her mother had ambitions for Mary to marry a professional—a doctor, lawyer, or businessman—certainly not a jazz musician. When Mary told her folks that she had secretly married me, her mom threw a fit and escorted Mary out of the house. Naturally, my big-hearted parents invited Mary to stay with them whenever she came home from school. Moms and Pops did the right thing by us. As had been the case with my parents, our children eventually won over Mary's folks.

On his way to the family gathering in North Carolina in late August, Pops took my Ellingtonian suggestion, "Drop Me off in Harlem" to heart. There I was, waving goodbye to him on the steps in front of the Coneys' apartment on 168th Street and Audubon Avenue. It was right around the corner from the old Audubon Ballroom, where, years later, Malcolm X would meet his untimely end.

I had five dollars in my pocket, a half-assed set of drums and cymbals, and a brown summer suit. But I felt as if I stood on the shoulders of all the musicians and teachers I had studied and played with in Chicago—from my family, neighborhood, and school bands.

I had no idea how the adventure would play out.

# PART 2

## *New York City, Jazz Mecca, 1957-1969*

# CHAPTER 11

## *Harlem, the Manhattan School of Music & Cafeteria*

I moved in with Bill Coney, his wife Hazel, and her family, the McPhersons, who enthusiastically adopted me. Her younger cousin Joe Rigby was already playing the saxophone when I met him. And he's still playing professionally all these years later.

It was my third stay at their place. My second stay was right after Tanglewood. I made my first stay when I was 21. Riley Gordon, a close friend, and I flew in on a new four-gas engine Constellation. We stayed with the Coneys for a week.

Their son Bill, about twelve years older than Riley and me, showed us around. Now, I lived here. I felt part of the family.

After learning my schedule of classes for the fall semester at the Manhattan School of Music, I got a night job as a janitor at the downtown offices of Montgomery Ward. I reported at 6 p.m. each weeknight and worked until 2 a.m., cleaning office cubicles in the block-long, triangular-shaped building that still stands there at the entrance of the Holland Tunnel. Some nights, I was assigned to clean the toilets on two of the four floors occupied by the company. It was a preferred assignment because the toilets were closed off from the open space of the whole floor. Neither the supervisor nor his assistant ever came in to check while we were working, whereas in the office space, someone was always watching. We joked about it, but we all needed the job—just enough not to get caught goldbricking.

Happy to have a job and a scholarship, to be living with the Coneys and starting my graduate studies, there were a few changes I had to make in my thinking. There's a long tradition of excellent Chicago musicians who left the Midwest to make their bones here; that trend continues to the present. Having grown up under the eye of so many older musicians who nudged me to New York, I inferred (or imagined) from their counsel that I would be leaving the racism endemic and systemic in Chi-town behind. Although I wanted it to be so, it was crazy thinking. For a jazz and classical musician, New York was the place to be, but I had to accept that I might find bigotry and hate anywhere.

My thinking about how to get work changed. Everything came relatively easy in Chicago because I knew so many musicians, thanks to my family, school bands, and large circle of friends. I had grown up in the game. By contrast, the New York scene then, perhaps even now, was extremely tight-knit and difficult to crack. The musicians' union and the school helped, but had it not been for the network of big brothers and sisters, fellow musicians, and new friends that I made, I might not have survived.

These folks were there for me from my first day at the Manhattan School of Music. Coleridge-Taylor Perkinson (Perk) was a brilliant composer-conductor who had just graduated from Manhattan. Perk introduced himself during that first week, and we remained close, musically and socially, for the rest of his life. He turned me on to a world of Black composers and classically-trained musicians. Many of these folks were looking for other talented Black musicians to be able to fit into certain situations. For instance, Black symphony orchestras were doing cotillions for Black socialites. They needed a timpanist, so I started getting side work.

The Manhattan School of Music was miles ahead in many ways. Trumpeter Donald Byrd was in my graduate class, working toward his doctorate in music education. His pioneering spirit helped inspire the academy to appreciate jazz as a subject worthy of study at the university level. He was among the first who established a jazz curriculum for college music departments.

In short, I was surrounded by inspiring people.

My final obstacle was my hubris. I was drowning in that Egyptian river, Denial. Despite my proficiencies in percussion in the classical music world, I was not as good a jazz drummer as I thought—at least not yet. There were no New York drummers in the U of I lexicon. Everybody who came to the Apple in those days could already play, and most were a lot better than me. That realization slapped me upside the head real fast and did wonders for my humility. I thought I was hot stuff because I could sight read fairly well. I was doing that every day and in many different styles, but I didn't yet know all the professional aspects of being a New York-style jazz drummer.

I was in the major leagues without the preparation of training camp. New York style is different from the Midwest, the South, and the West Coast; it's faster paced and more aggressive. No question, I was a sorry jazz player for a while. This lesson took time to sink in as folks I consistently underestimated continued to kick my ass on the bandstand.

My newfound friends from the Manhattan School of Music came to my aid and began to tutor me in bebop, which I had heard but never played seriously. My closest friends that first year were fellow percussion students—in particular, Eddie Cornelius and Phil Brown.

Seasoned professionals with lots of big band and small group experience, they were about five years older and native New Yorkers. They helped me adjust to the New York style of playing on top of the beat, quite different from Chicago swing and Mississippi Delta blues. It took me a decade to internalize the feeling so that it was second nature.

I had the mindset of a lifetime learner and was not above copying excellence. I soon played gigs as a percussionist in which I was stationed next to the drum kit. I studied the drummer's wrists, how they held the sticks, their movements and attitudes, particularly Charlie Persip and Philly Joe Jones (and later Tony Williams).

During that first fall semester at Manhattan, I rehearsed and performed with the school's orchestra and the percussion ensemble. Grad classes were often much easier than the undergrad work at U of I. I had already covered many subjects, but there were different references and terminology to adjust to. I teamed up with a couple of other students in the same quandary, Danny Holgate and Bill Phipps. By helping one another, we all got through with flying colors.

In addition to all of this help, one afternoon a week after classes, I attended a rehearsal with the National Training Orchestra, an amateur symphony orchestra at City Center on 55th Street. Mentored and conducted by Leon Barzan and later Franz Bibo, the orchestra helped familiarize us with the classical repertoire we might encounter during an audition. Members of the Met or Philharmonic percussion sections visited occasionally and gave us tips or shared tales of their professional lives. Professor Paul Price often told us that some of the most important information in our education came at such moments.

As I matured, the importance of shared experience, particularly the fraternity of percussion elders in the oral/aural tradition, became the foundation of my success. It helped me curb my arrogance, gain self-confidence, and endure the inevitable hardships of the music profession. Having had the opportunity to perform under a variety of styles, I learned to study conductors, their habits and idiosyncrasies. I discovered how to hear the inner rhythm of the orchestra and how to follow the conductor.

At any stage of one's performing career, a misunderstanding can lead to embarrassment and a complete loss of self-confidence. It's better to make mistakes and errors early in the game—and remember not to repeat them. Especially in New York, mistakes are long remembered. A silly habit easily becomes a reputation.

Among my most memorable mentors was the Manhattan School Symphony's musical director, Jonel Perlea. An incredibly clear and nuanced conductor, the French-born maestro had been the conductor of the prestigious orchestra, Suisse Romande. Conductors I had worked with at Illinois were more like generals than musicians. Perlea was demanding but also sensitive, continually challenging us. Once in the middle of a concert, there was a passage that he could never get us in the orchestra to play softly enough for his satisfaction during our weekly rehearsals. As we approached the passage, he looked directly at us and hid his baton behind his back. He looked right at us, so we didn't stop or hesitate, but it startled us so that we collectively gasped and whispered the passage. A smile broke out on the maestro's face as we realized he had tricked us into sounding more professional in the middle of a live performance. I use his idea now, and it's still highly effective.

Besides playing timpani in the orchestra, my scholarship job was running the school cafeteria. It was exactly what I had been doing throughout my undergraduate study at Illinois.

I wasn't shocked to find that all the other scholarship grad students had jobs in the library or business offices. I just didn't know to ask and took the first available option. But it was cool. I ate well at school, and we had lots of laughs. I recall the time I accidentally filled all the sugar dispensers with salt and the salt shakers with sugar. It took me a while to figure out why the diners said the coffee tasted strange and their vegetables tasted unusually sweet.

Since I ran the place, I decided not to fire myself.

# CHAPTER 12

## *Concerto for Marimba, Johnny Richards & West Side Story*

Though a Chicagoan by heart, I learned to adjust to the ways of New Yorkers.

I had help. For example, riding the subway back to Harlem from my job and school was like attending a jam session. Extemporaneous events often happened because people with obvious mental problems mixed with commuters and late-night revelers. I began to notice certain patterns.

One strange, stern-looking, dark-complexioned man in a black hat rode every night at the same time. When a white man in business attire walked by, the black-hatted man reacted violently, swinging his arm as if punching the air. All the regular riders knew him. No one ever sat beside him, even on weekends. But one Saturday morning, two young couples got on the train. There was only one empty seat left, the one beside this man. One brother offered the seat to the two young ladies and his friend, all of whom demurred.

At the next station, the door opened, and the stereotypical white businessman with an attaché case entered and walked by. Now you know all of us regulars were waiting for this unsuspecting guy to trigger Blackhat's vigorous reaction, which caused the polite young man to leap up and dance out of the way. Although we found it thoroughly entertaining that night, the sad part is that the "greatest" and "richest" country has never had adequate medical facilities to care for all those who need it. The same is true of the homeless among us.

We have the resources and the knowledge to help so many of the needy, but those with the will to do so are not in power.

The subway was particularly convenient because the train stopped right on 168th Street. The exit was just a few steps from the apartment entrance. Nevertheless, one night I managed to get stopped by the police, despite that short distance. Could it be that I was considered suspicious by law enforcement? In front of the building where I happened to be living?

During my second semester in New York, Mary joined me. She had her degree and wanted to work, so I took her to school and introduced her to Dean Whitford. He interviewed Mary and offered her a job as a school receptionist.

She enjoyed the gig and convinced me to quit my night job. I was more than okay with that; I was elated.

I prepared Paul Creston's Concerto for Marimba and Orchestra for my graduate recital and performed it that spring, accompanied by my friend and classmate, Zita Carno, who played the orchestra part on the piano. When she graduated from Manhattan School of Music, she took the piano chair with the Los Angeles Philharmonic and stayed until her retirement a few years ago. We had worked together before, performing Bela Bartok's *Sonata for Two Pianos and Percussion* earlier in the year, and I knew she was the right choice for the Creston concerto.

After that recital, the phone started to ring. Word was out.

Meanwhile, Mary and I moved from the Coneys' apartment to that of another of my mother's cousins, Addie Watson. She lived in a five-floor walk-up on Tinton Avenue in the Bronx, just down the street from Mount Morris High School. Why do I remember it so well?

I had to make my first few gigs walking my drums up the hill to 166th Street, then down and up the steps to the Third Avenue 'L,' and transfer to the subway at 149th Street to get to downtown Manhattan. Then, after the gig, I went back the same way late at night. Eventually, Mary and I found a kitchenette with a shared bathroom on West 82nd Street in the Upper West Side. From that point on, things gradually got better.

I performed jazz and classical music outside of grad school at the recommendation of my fellow students and friends. It was the foundation for establishing myself in the

New York music scene. My first jazz gig in New York was with guitarist Kenny Burrell at Minton's Playhouse.

Nevertheless, I was reluctant to put too much faith in gigging for a living. As if on cue, after I got my master's degree that May, I received my New York City teaching license in the mail and began work as a substitute teacher, in Music primarily, along with English at the junior high school level. Now that room and board were covered, I could prospect for work with greater selectivity.

If I had admitted to any ambitions before coming to the Apple, they included playing with the Sauter-Finnegan Orchestra and the Johnny Richards Orchestra. Both employed a full-time percussionist along with the regular drummer.

Trumpeter-drummer Eddie Sauter (who studied at Juilliard) and pianist Bill Finnegan (who studied at the Paris Conservatory) were big band arrangers who came together in 1952 to create a popular swing band that used innovative arrangements and often unusual instruments. Bandleader Johnny Richards (born Juan Manuel Cascales) arrived in New York in 1952 from Los Angeles. His forward-looking arrangements for the Stan Kenton Orchestra left no doubt about the influence of Duke Ellington.

I got the percussion chair for both bands because Phil Brown, one of my classmates at the Manhattan School, had the gig, but he wasn't quite ready. A couple of classmates recommended me. The jobs required a lot of timpani and sight-reading skills, so I fit right in. Little did I know at the time how valuable this exposure would be.

Even more compelling for a percussionist than these two well-known orchestras bridging the world of classical symphony music and the so-called jazz tradition was the recent hit that had just opened in 1957, *West Side Story*. Among the first Broadway musicals to have a percussion chair in addition to the drummer, it was much talked about among percussionists.

As it turned out, the show, like the two jazz orchestra percussion gigs, fell right into my lap. Good luck had stung me once more.

My friend and classmate from the U of I, Michael Colgrass, became the substitute percussionist for *West Side Story*. Mike was an excellent musician, but his first love was composition. He inspired me to write my first published composition for a percussion ensemble called Introduction and Samba when I was a sophomore at Illinois. At any rate, *West Side Story* needed a capable musician in the percussion chair to perform the last of the show's remaining dates on Broadway and then play the drum chair for the national touring company's unlimited run.

For context, as sweet as this tour looked and as ideal as it could be for me as a new jack, few working New York musicians wanted to go on the road. You could lose a lot of contacts. Contractors called you, and if you were unavailable a couple of times, they wouldn't continue calling. If the job is challenging, as this show certainly was, many less confident musicians wouldn't want to risk sullying their reputation. In

Mike's case, he had the skills, but touring meant time away from composing his music.

He called me and gave me a copy of the percussion score, which had a lot of tasty vibraphone solos in it. I liked that. I watched the performance for two weeks and memorized all the solo parts. When Mike left the show, I did the last seven weeks on Broadway at the Winter Garden. Meanwhile, I memorized the drum chair, which had its own solo parts and underlined all the choreography. When we finally took the show on the road, I knew the whole routine and managed to help the local percussionist in each city where we played.

Looking back over fifty years and almost fifty shows I did on Broadway, off Broadway, and off-off-Broadway, including a few as musical director, *West Side Story* was by far the most challenging show technically—in drum and percussion books. Ever so thoroughly orchestrated for the percussion players, it became my musical boot camp and a remarkable learning experience.

After those seven weeks in the Broadway orchestra pit, I heard what each individual musician played. Rather than concentrating on the music (manuscript), I listened and observed the movement on stage: the acting, singing, choreography, and even the audiences' reactions. It was a life-changing discovery. I began to understand my relationship with the whole production.

*West Side Story* was a masterful stroke of talented collaborators making musical theater history. Running for 732 performances before it even hit the road, the show was a politically engaging Modernist masterpiece. It was real life.

If you traded out the New York switchblades for Chicago's bombs, it could have been about my family's South Side story!

It was an old tale even when William Shakespeare penned his Romeo and Juliet.

But this team of musical pioneers had made it new. Leonard Bernstein—a classical music conductor, composer, and a jazz fan and advocate—wrote the music (the most requested excerpt for vibraphone at orchestral auditions is from this score). Stephen Sondheim made his Broadway debut as a lyricist. The book was by Arthur Laurents, and the show was directed and choreographed by Jerome Robbins, from the world of classical ballet.

It's not just that each element—singing, dancing, drama, music—was brilliant. How the many pieces worked together to achieve such artistry was the point. It was, as Duke Ellington said of the highest quality of art, "beyond category."

The play defined the era. It was a crisis about Italian-Puerto Rican cultures crossing borders on New York's West Side in 1957. But the whole country underwent a crisis about crossing borders. Three years earlier, the Supreme Court ruled that segregation was unconstitutional. But it didn't kill Jim Crow. Rather, Jim Crow kept killing us.

In 1955 our South Side neighbor Emmett Till was brutally tortured, lynched, and thrown in the Tallahatchie River for allegedly whistling at a white woman down in the Mississippi Delta while on summer vacation. But his death produced what one might call strange fruit: the struggle of everyday Black Americans to achieve basic human rights was front page news worldwide.

I was one minute out of graduate school and the only Black musician in the orchestra. I was hired to play the cross-country tour, but I had never been west of Illinois.

# CHAPTER 13

## *Section Leader, National Tour & Road Benefits*

Our first stop was Denver, Colorado, to play on July 1, 1959.

Everybody checked into a hotel adjacent to the theater. I asked the doorman where the Black people were. He directed me to a location called Five Points. It wasn't far from downtown and the theater. I checked into a decent-looking hotel, signed in, walked up to my room, and put my bag on the bed to unpack.

I heard some lively music coming from a nearby room. It turned out to be from the door next to mine. I knocked, the music stopped, and a gentleman in a shirt and necktie opened the door. It was J.J. Johnson. He was there with his quintet for the week, playing at the jazz club just up the block.

Like bandleaders Dizzy Gillespie, Betty Carter, and Art Blakey, among others, J.J. Johnson was old school. He ran his own jazz studies program for the next generation of talent. He had guys my age and younger in his group: Cedar Walton on piano, Spanky DeBrest on bass, Albert "Tootie" (now Kuumba) Heath on drums, and my homie Clifford Jordan on tenor saxophone. He took them on the road and passed on the music and culture to these hungry young cats. For me, it was an unexpected treat.

So every night after *West Side Story*, people knew where I had gone.

Those ten days in Denver were a great way to start my first road tour. I met percussionist and timpanist Walter Light from the Denver Symphony. *West Side Story* turned out to be a magnet. Everywhere it played, it drew all the prominent percussionists. They had to check it out. I met so many talented musicians. I was new to this world, and being around these professionals was highly beneficial.

Those of us in the road band flew to our next stop, Los Angeles. The cast and crew traveled on the company train with all the scenery and equipment. We cabbed directly to the venue to start rehearsing with the L.A. orchestra. Our musical director, Joseph Lewis, conducted. Stanley Keene was the associate conductor and pianist. Griff Howe was the guitarist. I was the drummer. First violinist-concertmaster Anton, first trumpet Godfrey (Sam) Shram, and first reed

Wally Kane led their sections. The seven of us rehearsed the details of phrasing and articulation and helped clarify the cues.

We had one whole day of rehearsal; after that, we performed the show live. With excellent leadership throughout the strings, reeds, brass, and rhythm section, the transfer proved seamless from city to city. One might expect that an orchestra from a large urban population might have a superior sound to those from smaller cities, but the musicianship was quite consistently up to the Broadway standard.

Nevertheless, every show was slightly different in some way. There was always something that I could improve on or correct for the next show. A continual learning mindset makes it possible to focus on the same material a thousand times and still find a challenge. The seven of us in the road band and the stagehands knew all the dialogue, dance moves, and lyrics to every tune. If anything went wrong in any small detail, we all noticed.

The repetition of performing it established a profound discipline in me. Being a section leader made me more tuned in as a sideman and an accompanist. The strictness of a touring show was like a graduate school in performance. The experiences I had gained playing in military bands were now coming in handy. All of my training was well-spent.

I liked L.A. and decided to rent a kitchenette for a couple of weeks near Beverly Hills. On my first night with free time, I took a stroll to check out the neighborhood and enjoy its architecture. I got stopped shortly thereafter by the police. They told me that folks in this town didn't take walks.

I found Shelly's Mann Hole and saw Shelly Manne and his band live. It was another great lesson in musicianship. Shelly played brushes so delicately and tastefully, yet everything was audible. He showed me that you don't have to pound to be heard clearly.

After those first two weeks, my cousin, Frances Cloud, and her husband, Hamilton, invited me to their home. They lived in Leimert Park, a quiet residential neighborhood near the campus of USC. I moved in with their family for the next few weeks. Fran and Hamp and their three children—Hamilton, Teri, and Leslie—provided the family atmosphere that I thrive in. Nevertheless, even in this environment, I managed to find some trouble to get my young self into.

One afternoon, after the matinee performance, I stopped to have a drink before dinner with one of the veteran actors and some of the stagehands. By this time, I had deluded myself into thinking I could hold my liquor, but I was out of my league with these cats. They were all at least forty years old. I was in my middle twenties and thought I was a grown man. Someone bought a round, and then I bought one. The next thing I knew, I had been taken over by "tee many martoonies," and it was time for the evening show. I hadn't eaten anything, and I was drunk as a skunk. The cats brought me back and put me in the pit. I don't remember playing the show that night. But afterward, I was sober enough to drive back to my cousins' house. They were also having a party, so I fit right in.

The next night the conductor chewed me out. He insisted that he and I had dinner together on matinee days. I was restricted to one drink at dinner time before shows. I realized that my behavior might cost many people a lot of money and waste a lot more folks' valuable time. That brought me to my senses.

Of course, that one episode labeled me as having a drinking problem with many music contractors in Los Angeles. Throughout the music industry, alcoholism is tolerated by many, as some in the profession did or do have that problem. I did not wish to be identified as a problem, so I was happy to accept the reprimand and assert more discipline upon myself. It doesn't take much to earn a bad reputation, and it always takes years to live one down. After that experience, I was more careful about who I hung out with. We got through the rest of the run without any further incidents. Lesson learned.

Mary met me at the end of the run in L.A. It was a thrill to be reunited. We were off to San Francisco for the next six weeks. The seven section leaders in the road band flew in a day early while Mary traveled with the show on the company train.

She and I enjoyed San Francisco. It was a great town for our reunion; we had a lot of fun. Mary spent a month there and then went back home to New York. I hung out a few times at a popular jazz club called Bop City and sat in with some local cats. I lived in a transient hotel next to the venue. Located at the base of Nob Hill, it catered to traveling theater people. On the road in those days, such an apartment cost all of $25 a week.

One afternoon I decided to go to Fisherman's Wharf on the other side of the hill and have dinner. I left my wallet on the dresser and had only pocket change when the bill came. I explained to the manager and asked if he'd let me get my wallet and come back. I gave him all my change before I realized I had to climb Nob Hill. Going up was rough, but the descent just about ruined me. I was sore for a week after that.

I found out that vibraphonist Cal Tjader was playing in town. When I got there, I saw Willie Bobo, whom I knew from hanging out at sessions in New York. Willie played drums and timbales. Mongo Santamaria was on the congas. Al McKibbin was the bassist, and the pianist was Lonnie Hewett. Most people will tell you that this was the best band Cal ever had.

I was there almost every night until *West Side Story*'s run ended.

Hearing a great jazz set (or two) after finishing our show was an added benefit of the road. It was music I could relax into and explore; it was renewal, a return to the source.

# CHAPTER 14

## *Chicago Reunited, The Lamplighter & Lloyd Price*

The next stop on the tour was Chicago for a six-month stay.

At that time, Moms was working for the Chicago Housing Authority. Having access to the city files on vacant apartments for limited lease, she found us a great apartment in the South Shore section close to the lake. Mary liked what she saw and secured the place. However, I knew the neighborhood was hostile to Black people, even those who only visited that section of the beach, much less lived there.

Mary was not obviously Black in appearance, but when I showed up, the landlord suddenly found a reason not to rent the place to us. It may have been a to-die-for crib, but none of us would die to live there. Moms found us another place right down the street from our old apartment on Drexel Blvd, which our uncle, cousins, and sometimes my brother Frank (who made his mark in the visual arts) occupied.

Our apartment building was between the Sutherland Hotel and Lounge on 47th Street and the building that the Black AF of M, Local 208, owned farther south. One of our neighbors on the first floor of the building was Rafael Donald Garret, a bassist, bass clarinetist, and a graduate of DuSable High School. I caught live groups at the Sutherland and numerous other clubs after I got home from the show or on nights off.

We hadn't been away long enough to forget the Windy City, so I just slipped right back into my South Side scene. It was great to be back home for an extended spell. The white AF of M, Local 10, was shocked to find I was already a Chicago's Black Local 208 member. I avoided the extra tax placed on traveling musicians. I didn't play around. I had my papers in order, so they had to acknowledge it.

Back then, a Black musician rarely (close to never) got the opportunity to do a Broadway show or orchestral symphony. The only exceptions were shows with a Black genesis and an all-Black cast. Three come to mind. The first two are operas with a Black twist.

*The Swing Mikado*, a parody of a Gilbert & Sullivan comic opera, first opened in 1938 in Chicago, then hit Broadway. *Carmen Jones* was a 1943 production that reimagined Georges Bizet's opera *Carmen* (with lyrics and book by Oscar

Hammerstein II) in a World War Two era, African American setting. But the real home run on Broadway was *Shuffle Along*, a 1921 production with music and lyrics by Eubie Blake and Noble Sissle. It ran for over 500 performances and spawned nine all-Black Broadway musicals over the next three years.

Returning to Chicago with a Broadway-based steady gig was a bold-ass victory. I considered my string instructor's admonition just two and a half years earlier that there was no work for a Negro in classical or Broadway music. Since my complexion hadn't changed, he must have wondered how I had gotten over it. I wasn't seeking vengeance (maybe a little) so much as hoping that Black talent now had a chance.

It would have been difficult to be the sole African American breaking through, but I wasn't alone. I was part of a generation of composers and players returning the Broadway musical to its roots in Black music. Instrumentalists from the classical world covered a wide range of Black popular music that would soon be in demand, thanks to shows like *West Side Story*. Little did I know at the time that I would get the call to play many of these shows because of having toured with *West Side Story*.

After that six-month run in Chicago, we were booked in Detroit for the next two weeks. The schedule then called for a series of shorter engagements, which meant a lot of moving of luggage and equipment and ourselves. It seemed like a good time to leave the tour, so I turned in my notice after Detroit and returned to New York.

Mary, our first daughter Lynn, and I lived in an apartment on the Upper West Side on the corner of 108th Street and Broadway. There was a Catholic school and a public school on the block. Public transportation was convenient. It was small but comfortable for the three of us.

As for working my hustle, I felt ready for anything New York threw at me. A year and a half of doing *West Side Story* around the country eight times a week had been my initiation into the life. I had road chops!

Touring with that show as a performer and section leader gave me a quiet confidence beyond any previous experience on stage or in school. I learned to deliver my best in a show that required my best night in and night out. Despite whatever else was going on in my life, I brought it for every audience. Struggles in my own life gave my performances more grit and gravitas.

I was serving the music, as they say, and the music was about to serve me.

The reputation I had garnered from that tour attracted the attention of composers from many genres. There was a shortage of Black percussionists at that time in New York. The few who were available were too busy to be always accessible. I met Gordon "Specs" Powell, the first Black studio musician (percussionist) at CBS, David Panama Francis, famed rock, R&B, and jazz drummer in the Fifties, Herbie Lovelle, the ultimate first call rock drummer, and (Samuel) "Sticks" Evans, Langston Hughes' percussionist and drummer for Prestige. They began to call me to sub for them in the studio and on the bandstand. I also subbed in other Broadway shows, which required learning the music and the cues. It was intense work but an excellent experience.

However, none of the music I was called upon to play was as difficult as what I had already been exposed to with Professor Paul Price's percussion ensemble, Harry Partch, the Manhattan School of Music, or *West Side Story*. Looking back after seven decades in the game, I see how formative these early experiences were. The thoroughness of this preparation allowed me to cross borders and "infiltrate" (desegregate) genres, bringing uptown skills downtown and vice versa.

My return to the percussion chair with the Johnny Richards Orchestra was the other calling card that got me studio work. Many of the musicians in the band were well connected in recording jobs and other bands. Their recommendations enabled me to join the staff orchestra at the American Broadcasting Company for radio and TV in 1962.

The Jimmy Dean Show had some bright moments. One featured act was Homer and Jethro, a fiddle and banjo duet. Known as the thinking man's hillbillies, they looked, dressed, and played country. They were also jazz musicians, influenced by gypsy guitarist Django Rinehardt—hot jazz and bop. We had a lot of fun jamming with them in rehearsals.

By the time ABC launched the Les Crane and Nipsey Russell Shows, we were a fifty-piece orchestra. The gig lasted until 1967, when all the staff orchestras left New York and moved to Los Angeles. But that steady income enabled me to buy a house in Long Island and raise my family.

I kept learning, especially on the drum kit, or the multiple percussion instrument (MPI), as Max Roach called it.

Gerald "Sonny" Brown, the longtime drummer with Rahsaan Roland Kirk, schooled me on how to project energy without becoming fatigued or running out of breath. Alan Dawson, Booker Ervin's drummer, showed me how, with kinetic energy, to conserve effort, think, and project the energy in a linear fashion. I had run track in high school and college, but now I took it upon myself to condition my body through strenuous exercise and controlled disciplined practice.

In those years, there were many situations to play in: recordings, show clubs with house bands, bars with a trio, venues on the Theater Owners Booking Association circuit, and private parties. In addition, each borough had its own scene; Brooklyn musicians didn't come to Manhattan and vice versa, except on special occasions. Uptown musicians didn't need to go downtown, but a lot of downtown musicians came uptown to hang out. Clubs in Harlem thrived. Many of them brought in headliners for weeks at a time. On Sundays, they might do a matinee. On weekdays there were jam sessions until 2 or 3 a.m., with young aspirants waiting in line for a chance to be heard. Once you passed the test, you usually worked on weekends, at least until a better situation arose.

Phil Brown and Eddie Cornelius, my percussion buddies, helped me find gigs and weekend club dates. Some were one-shot wonders; others went on for three or four nights a week. Some lasted months. Two gigs stand out as representative of those early years in New York.

The first was at The Lamplighter, and that job never seemed to end. Located in Valley Stream, Long Island, just across the New York City border in Nassau County, the club was equidistant between Aqueduct Racetrack in Queens County and Belmont Racetrack in Nassau County. Thus, it was the hangout spot for racing fans, bookies (pre-off track betting), gamblers, jockeys, wise guys, and various celebrities.

Mike Tuzzo and his wife Rose owned it. Mike hired a regular duo and added me as a weekend drummer. The show included a featured singer, sometimes a comedian, and occasionally a horn player. Our leader was the bassist Frank "Webb" Izzo; the pianist was Johnny Quinn, who was blind. Frank and I sometimes switched instruments. I knew the changes to more tunes than he did, and when Frank played drums, he sounded pretty good. He knew how to play the bass drum on all four beats and accent the high-hat cymbals.

Johnny had an incredible memory for songs, but every now and then, we got a request that stumped us. One night, a fairly lit-up patron came up and asked Johnny to do a title none of us knew. The customer insisted that we try, and he pressed a couple of bucks into Johnny's hand. We improvised a nice little song that everyone applauded. But the guy returned and indignantly demanded his tip back. Johnny reached into his pocket and returned the two bucks, which the guy then burned up with his lighter. We just stood there and laughed at this jelly-apple Maryland farmer (jelly = jive; apple = ass... as Jon Hendricks would say).

Crazy as it was, the gig lasted more than two years, and I mean every weekend.

The second job was one I never wanted to end. It was with Lloyd Price, the R&B vocalist from New Orleans. He had moved to New York after his million-selling hits like "Lawdy Miss Clawdy" and was known as Mr. Personality because of his 1959 hit single, "Personality." His twelve-piece band played at Lloyd Price's Turntable at 1674 Broadway. The club was named after his new label.

Lloyd had seen me conduct and lead my band Composer's Workshop Ensemble, and that's what he needed from me five nights a week. I conducted. We didn't play Monday and Sunday nights. New York did not allow nightclubs to be open on Sunday nights in those days. I managed to do double duty. I taught music in school during the day and led the band at night.

I loved the gig. I only left because things got too hot. Logan, who was Black and more Lloyd's bodyguard than a manager, didn't show up for work one day. The police found his body. He had been shot to death in the upstairs office. Having antagonized a member of the Mafia, he now had a hole in his head. I don't know how much attention it got in the news, but we musicians knew what was up.

Going into disfavor with powerful (and unstable) people can produce unpredictable outcomes. Another lesson learned.

# CHAPTER 15

## *Jingles, Demos, Records & Composer's Workshop Ensemble*

Coinciding with percussion work on Broadway shows and drum work on club dates, an additional opportunity opened up in the recording studio. During the late Fifties and into the early years of the Sixties, a whole industry of Black music was getting recorded in Manhattan: jazz, R&B, soul, pop, and film score material. Many out-of-towners came to record on weekends, including producers from Detroit, Chicago, and Philadelphia.

These record dates were usually under scale pay for union rules, but the income was not reported. Before Motown and Philly International were established business entities, these producers brought their young artists to work with Big Apple studio musicians and arrangers. I remember doing several sessions with Gladys Knight and the Pips, among others. We called these sessions "demos," as in demonstration recordings, a vehicle to get the attention of commercial record labels.

The demos led me to more recordings: individual songs, complete albums, film scores, and TV commercials. I had been 'buked and scorned by Ole Miss rednecks at Ike's inauguration in '53 for playing timpani while being Black. But now music arrangers in the Big Apple were happy to find me, a Black percussionist with conservatory training and knowledge of Black music and culture. As Mahalia Jackson sang, "It was howdy-howdy and never-never goodbye."

Once again, I was in the right place at the right time. And I kept an open mind.

The television commercials, for example, were a trip. We had an hour to record 57 seconds of music, which left 3 seconds to voice over, "Buy some at your local drugstore," in the one-minute slot TV provided. Although they kept it simple for the most part, it takes skill to sight read music you've never seen before. At times what they wanted was pretty insipid, but they paid us to play it, not rearrange it. Musicians on these record dates rarely made mistakes. We focused on the music and took the job seriously. Being around such artists was a privilege for me, young and new on the scene. No question, the atmosphere, skill level, and team spirit helped me to play my best.

I never knew who would show up. These one-minute ditties often featured star vocalists. I remember recording a Coca-Cola commercial, and there was Marvin Gaye and Tammy Terrell singing the jingle!

The money was a bit tricky. We got residual payments (though they were minuscule) for the ad's run on television. However, for some of the more prolific studio musicians, these payments over a year added up to hundreds or thousands of dollars. As one might expect, only a few Black musicians were in this elite group. That's not because of a lack of talent, but rather because they had no control over hiring musicians for a TV commercial, Broadway production, album recording, film score, or TV show. That job fell to a select clique of contractors. Occasionally, a show produced by a Black entity installed a Black contractor and a majority of Black musicians. Rarely are more than two such shows produced on Broadway simultaneously. Some, like *The Wiz* and *The Lion King*, may last a few years, but those are few and far between.

Though I was glad to get this studio work, it wasn't steady and dependable yet. The money was supplemental, and that was good. More importantly, the experience was formative and helped put me on the map.

In 1959, I made my first New York recording playing percussion on *Walk Softly, Run Wild* as a member of Johnny Richards Orchestra. I played on some great jazz recordings in the early Sixties as well: with Charles Mingus, *The Complete Town Hall Concert*; with Jimmy Smith, *Monster*; with J.J. Johnson, *Broadway Express*; with Herbie Mann, *Our Mann Flute*; with Jack McDuff, *A Change Is Gonna Come*; with Sy Oliver and his orchestra, *Easy Walker*; with

Michel Legrand, *Michel Legrand Big Band Plays Richard Rodgers*; and *My Fair Lady, My Way* with Johnny Richards and his orchestra.

In terms of live shows, I played on a lot of original works by contemporary composers.

The music was often accompanied by dancers, whether a recital or an off-Broadway production in Harlem, the West Village, or the Lower East Side. All my training in percussion came in handy.

In 1959, I began Composer's Workshop Ensemble, my working band for sixty-plus years. The group has had at least nine or ten players consistently and has evolved, depending on the availability of musicians. Rarely have the same people played for every performance.

One of the few disadvantages of being in New York is that everyone's always busy, but I easily make personnel changes when the compositions call for it. For instance, we might need an unusual voice like a particular sax or tuba, Asian instruments, or additional percussion. All these options are a phone call away. We work primarily in New York, Washington, D.C., and sometimes in Philadelphia. The band plays both my musical compositions and my arrangements of tunes by Aretha Franklin, the Beatles, or Steve Wonder, for example. We have recorded six albums produced by Strata-East, Baystate, Miff Music, and Engine Studios.

In 1961, I found a home for Composer's Workshop Ensemble when I opened a music studio with my two oldest New York friends and fellow composers, Perk and Jack Jeffers. I met both during my first week in New York—Perk at the Manhattan School of Music and Jack at the National Training Orchestra at City Center. Jack was in the Army at the time, stationed at Fort Dix, New Jersey. A multifaceted individual, he worked as an aeronautical engineer before becoming a full-time musician. At age forty, he entered law school, graduated two years later, and passed the bar exam in New York. We've played in symphony orchestras, smaller ensembles, and shows on and off Broadway. When I started my group, Jack became, and still is, my bass trombonist. When he formed the New York Classic Big Band, I was, and still am, his drummer.

As a family man, having a place to rehearse outside the home environment proved to be more necessity than luxury. Our rehearsal-performance space was a five-floor walkup with a shared bathroom west of 10th Avenue. Having taken over the lease from a violinist friend, Marie Hence, the rent, $44 per month, was a scuffle for us. I started doing Broadway shows again about this time so I could afford to take over the whole nut but barely.

Getting that real estate happened just in time. From the moment we opened, I kept meeting and playing with people pushing experimental music's envelope. They were important composers whose styles varied greatly and were often complicated and intriguing. They dealt with free improvisation and navigated new and different approaches for musicians. I adopted a model of continual improvement and kept learning. Two experiences stand out as markers of the era.

The first one was with drummer Charlie Persip. Five years my senior, Charlie taught me how to analyze orchestral scores and big band jazz styles in the context of recorded music. He had played and recorded with Dizzy Gillespie, toured with Billy Eckstine as his drummer and conductor, and taught drums through the Jazz Mobile program in Harlem and later at the music department at the New School. He passed away in August 2020 at the age of 91. Charlie was an equally important drum teacher in my evolution, along with my first drum teacher Oliver S. Coleman in Chicago and Professor Paul Price at the University of Illinois in Urbana-Champaign. What these three taught me formed the foundation of my success as a professional musician, composer, and arranger.

The second experience was a baptism by fire into the New Thing.

My baptizer was none other than my old childhood buddy from 58th Street: Maurice McIntyre, one of the doo-wop singing kids in our apartment building. Now named Kalaparush Ara Difda, he had returned to New York to live after a long hiatus in Chicago. He had been a student of my dad's and had become involved in the early development of the Association for the Advancement of Creative Musicians (AACM). A highly influential group of pioneering musicians and composers, the AACM combined music with visual art, dance, and theater. They stretched the boundaries of the jazz tradition and incorporated elements of avant-garde and "free" improvisation, or "outside" music.

In Kalaparush, I found a soulmate who matched my energy and pushed me to match his energy. In those years, I was the percussionist in the staff orchestra at ABC, just playing written music and doing live shows, sometimes five nights a week, sometimes two days a week. The charts were constricting and measured. And playing free improvised music with Kalaparush influenced the energy input I had to invest in my approach to my instrument.

It made a physical difference. My conditioning changed. I got stronger and technically more proficient. I started playing almost daily at the studio with him.

Everything I knew about drumming changed. He lit a fire under my ass. Like William Blake, he knew that "energy is eternal delight." He was the influence I needed to counter my staff job as a flat business guy who just read and played musical scores. I became a more inventive musician and composer. I tapped into this other, more energetic part of myself, which I think might have prolonged my life.

In many ways, he prepared me for Ken McIntyre and Sam Rivers to enter my life. I wound up working with both of them over the next thirty years on a fairly regular basis. They were certainly taking the New Thing in some new directions.

Kenneth Arthur (Makanda) McIntyre called me at the studio because Jack Jeffers told him I could read music fluently. We clicked instantly when I saw Ken's music. It was measured and meticulous in its framework, but as I soon found out, he encouraged me to go outside and break those boundaries. And he broke them as well. While he was strict in how far he wanted you to go, he still gave me that avenue.

I joined his quartet, which included Bross Townsend on piano and Ernie Farrow (the older brother of Alice Coltrane, née McCloud) on bass, with Ken on saxophones. He lived in the Bushwick section of Brooklyn on Quincey Street with his wife and two young sons. We rehearsed regularly once a week after school, played a number of local gigs, and recorded *Year of the Iron Sheep* for RCA Victor in 1962.

After a while, Ed Stout replaced Bross, and Reggie Workman replaced Ernie. We were all living in Brooklyn at the time. Brooklyn has its own culture, different than that of Manhattan. It had a slower, more relaxed pace. It felt more like Chicago to me.

The year before, Ken had recorded an album with Eric Dolphy, leading to some artistic experimental music and unique associations. Ken got us a gig at a house party on 54th Street, near the famous Birdland, just off Broadway, at a small five-story building. We set up on the second floor overlooking the opulent staircase landing. It was exotically carpeted with a large bench under a huge abstract painting on the wall. Looking at it for a while, I thought it was something Salvador Dali might do. Moments later, I looked down again, and this elegantly dressed dude sat there looking up at the band. He had a wild-ass, looong handlebar moustache. It was Dali. Ken's friend who hired us was Andy Warhol.

Like Kalaparush, Ken helped me escape the rigidity that formal musical education had instilled in me and traditional structures of the swing music that I grew up with. He composed using unusual or irregular rhythm patterns, changing meters, and dissonant melodic and chordal passages. He created new ways of presenting musical ideas.

Once, in a piece he composed after the death of Malcom X, he asked me to put my drumsticks down and express how I felt about the assassination. On another occasion, he asked if I could play "time" without a measured meter! I don't think anyone else ever thought to ask that of me musically, but I've used the device ever since when I think it fits.

I continued to play with Ken and his quartet through the mid-Seventies. Eventually, my student, Napoleon Revels-Bey, replaced me. Ken and I also worked together as university professors in a unique program he created.

During the last two decades of his life, Ken made a trip to Africa. While in Zaire, he was given the name Makanda (meaning many skins or many heads), which he used for the rest of his life. Today there is an active organization called The Makanda Project, which continues to perform his compositions, some of which were never recorded during his lifetime.

He left us in 2001, having completed his 70th year on the planet.

# CHAPTER 16

## *Nina Simone, Harry Belafonte & Among School Children*

In the early Sixties, in addition to teaching, recording, and playing locally, I began touring with top-level talent across the country. I worked summers and occasionally took a semester off to tour with an artist, provided the salary compensated my loss of income teaching. Two musicians stand out in my memory as definitive examples of that Jim Crow (pre-1965) period.

Nina Simone was my first professional road gig with a big-name star. And what an introduction. Here was this classically trained pianist, playing her songs and covers that had become pop favorites. Her repertoire included her cover of "I Loves You, Porgy," which hit big in 1958. But by 1964, in response to two 1963 events in Mississippi—the murder of Medgar Evers in Jackson and the bombing of the 16th Street Baptist Church in Birmingham that killed four young Black girls—Nina composed and performed "Mississippi Goddam" and released it as a single. The song was so direct, audacious, and powerful that it became an unofficial anthem for the civil rights era. Using pop music as a platform for change, she seized the day.

As a Black female singer-songwriter-bandleader, Nina was a pioneer who wove her blend of gospel, R&B, jazz, blues, folk, classical, and pop styles. There was no one like her. But after a while, I began to see a certain frustration. This incredible, crowd-pleasing artist could not get a job in classical music because she was Black. That bugged her, big time. She never hesitated to show off her piano virtuosity because she had no opportunity to express that side of herself. Consider "To Be Young, Gifted and Black," the song she would later write at the end of the decade with Weldon Irvine, her musical director. She turned despair into hope: that was her genius.

I met her through Rodger Sanders, known in music as Montego Joe, a fantastic conga player from Montego Bay and historian of African drumming. A friend of mine from the Manhattan School of Music, he started working with Nina when he finished his degree. When her drummer, Bobby Hamilton, split suddenly, Roger called me and asked if I could sub. We did a couple of local gigs, and everything seemed all right. But on tour, things got heavy. Despite (or because of) her incredible talent, she could sometimes be temperamental. Tempestuous is more like it. In your face.

I had never dealt with that level of explosiveness in a bandleader. All kinds of things happened—not just on the bandstand but sometimes in the dressing room. I was not used to being called out, snapped at, provoked, or blamed for something I didn't do. I discovered that I could be cantankerous in response. I look back now and see what a young chump-ass fool I was (she was a year younger than me). Instead of biting my lip, I kept biting her bait. She kept reeling me in until I got wise.

Still, bickering was one thing; protecting Nina from her husband was another. None of us in the band wanted to take sides, only ensure Nina's safety. Andy Stroud, her husband-manager, was a New York City police detective. No question, Andy was absolutely the nicest guy in the world if you knew how to be cool. We all knew how to be cool, but Nina sometimes forgot.

I remember one occasion in particular, a seriously wrong time to forget. We were in Florida. I'm talking pre-Rosa Parks—that is to say, segregated, "back of the bus." Florida was not a place Black folks could expect a fair shake should law enforcement chance upon any ruckus.

Despite the circumstances (or because of them), Andy and Nina, as lovers (and business teams) sometimes do, got into a disagreement. A storm of swirling threats ensued, and from inside our bungalow, we heard it escalate into a tornado. It was most definitely the right time to be cool, and some of us in the band calmly walked over to their bungalow. Without taking sides, we interceded before anything got crazy. But that was my last tour with Nina Simone.

Oddly, the moment I left her tour, Bobby Hamilton returned. I subbed for him now and then in New York, but I never went on the road with Nina again. Although the music was magic, adapting to the unpredictable grew exhausting. For some people, constant tumult is fuel, or at least nothing to get hung up about. For me, the most diplomatic way of saying it is that touring with Nina sweetened my return to Mary, our daughters, and our familial peace of mind.

Harry Belafonte was on the other side of the spectrum. His rise to fame was meteoric and from multiple directions. Seven years older than me, he was unstoppable. His 1956 album, *Calypso* (and the song "Day-O"), was a best seller. He brought the music of Trinidad and the Caribbean into white American homes. I knew how influential he had been in Hollywood in the 1950s, especially getting *Carmen Jones*, *Bright Road*, and *Island in the Sun*, all with Dorothy Dandridge, made. Those films showed Black people the way we really are. How could one not feel, as Sam Cooke put it, a change is gonna come?

Harry exuded charisma. In his presence, I felt that anything was possible. He was tuned in and more than just good looking. He proved to be the epitome of a race man, the corrective to the media portrait of Black manhood as servile, stupid, and simple. A great theater and screen actor, he understood his role as a border crosser and cultural pioneer.

His level of success was proof, but like the great ones, his appeal transcended every category.

Had acting been his only contribution to American culture, it would have been enough. But he took it further as a musical performer. I can attest. I did several national tours and many recording sessions and TV dates with him. His command of his material was off the charts. His leadership of the band and the tour was inspired.

Had song been his only contribution to American culture, it would have been enough. But perhaps his greatest gift was how he leveraged his skills behind the scenes, not only in Hollywood but in Washington, D.C., and later with Africa and the United Nations. It was not until many years later that I learned that Harry was a sponsor and fundraiser for the Civil Rights Movement. A close friend of Martin Luther King, Jr., Harry went on to serve as a UNICEF goodwill ambassador. Like my father, Harry is tuned into a higher moral frequency. Playing in his band was something else.

These experiences with world-class performers inspired me, and my enthusiasm for the music was something I brought with me into the classroom. After every tour, I had work awaiting me with the Board of Ed. I maintained my designation as a "temporary substitute" because, if I accepted the "regular substitute" status, I could be assigned to a specific school with an obligation to be there five days a week, which limited my music opportunities. My ace in the hole was John Motley, a former classmate at Manhattan School of

Music. A fine choral director and composer, John was the assistant director of junior high school music in New York City. Whenever I came back from a tour, I called John. By the time I got to his office in Brooklyn, he had found me a position teaching in a predominately Black school. That was where I was needed and where I most wanted to be.

I remember one of the assignments most vividly: The Sterling School, located on Sterling and Vanderbilt Streets in Brooklyn, right below the big traffic circle at Grand Army Plaza. Mary worked there as well. It was a 600 school—that is, a place where all the students had been kicked out of other schools. I found that the kids were not thugs, but they were smarter than the teachers they were encountering. Some got thrown out because they were too inconvenient.

A lot of those alleged problem students became life-long friends. Mary and I cornered one middle schooler with a big mouth and a bigger attitude. We discovered that he couldn't read; nobody had ever taught him the alphabet. So we came into school an hour early and worked with him and a few other kids. I don't know how far he went, but he was reading by the time he left us. He opened my eyes to the sociological problems many children experience. A lack of service to these kids was so often the real problem.

In that first year as a substitute teacher, I quickly learned that professional jealousy was a disease with some teachers, especially those who were frustrated musicians, writers, or actors. I could not get everyone a recording gig or a tour, nor could I turn them into first-call musicians. Hence, my conversation with them focused entirely on school, not my adventures on the road or in the studio.

I got better (and grew smarter) at juggling many jobs. Whenever a decision arose over a gig, Mary and I always discussed the options in terms of what was best for the family. Music was my first love, but family was my first responsibility. Like any married couple with children, we had our share of economic difficulties and hardships, but those were temporary problems that we managed to find our way through.

Mary and I grew up in the last years of the Great Depression. As had been the case for our parents, the strength of our family relationships enabled us to raise and educate our children. If something happened or someone passed away, our family was there to comfort one another. In this sense, the rest of the world was strange to us. The standard of moral support that we were given was what bound our family together. Everybody was family. A lot of us were weird at times, and there were some hot tempers, but the wiser and more mature folks kept everything together.

There's a term called being raised right. That means being taught at an early age how to treat people, in general. It was rare back then to see someone display the selfish attitude so prevalent of late. I wonder if it will take another depression or breakdown in the social order to return us to a more caring society.

As for my choices regarding being on the bandstand and in the classroom, some of the cats challenged me: "Are you a teacher or a musician?" I didn't fall for their either-or logic because I was good at both and liked doing both. I'm sure that performing music regularly made me a better music teacher. I brought to the classroom my whole life as a working musician. Who I am as a teacher or as a human being is inseparable from the music I make. As William Butler Yeats wrote in "Among School Children," "How can we know the dancer from the dance?"

From 1957 to '67, I taught junior high school Music and English as a substitute teacher. As a member of the musician's union at an early age, I knew the advantages of collective action. That's why I played an active part in forming a teacher's union. Throughout the five boroughs, standards, resources, and levels of learning varied greatly. We brought it up again and again; nothing happened. Once we all refused to go to work, we got the necessary compliance. All this went down before the American Federation of Teachers was founded.

While balancing touring and teaching with playing record dates and club dates, I took a lot of bad or low-paying gigs, yet I learned something from every situation. No experience, whether teaching in the classroom or playing music, was wasted.

Looking back now, none of us foresaw in the early Sixties that the music I loved and lived my whole life would be admitted into the university curriculum before the decade ended.

Those of us Black teachers working in the schools had been sneaking bits and pieces of our culture into the minds of our students. For example, the regular curriculum for junior high school at that time included songs of the antebellum South—Steven Collins Foster ditties about happy and contented slaves. Now I knew my students didn't want to hear or revisit any of that. It might fly in an all-white neighborhood school, but it went nowhere with us. I snuck in a popular song we all listened to at home, like Ben E. King's "Stand by Me," and we all sang together.

When my General Music classes stopped having severe discipline problems, the associate principals came to the music room and checked me out. Gradually the whole atmosphere changed. Tensions dissolved. Students got more involved and thoroughly enjoyed the class, but the administrators criticized me for getting too close to the students.

This model of the instructor as a detached and objective, all-knowing authority transmitting knowledge onto the empty mind screens of their students was dead wrong. Learning happens in the exchange of knowledge, so it's valuable for the student to feel free to exchange. Why put the instructor on a pedestal?

My professors in music education at U of I and the Manhattan School of Music also subscribed to this notion of the teacher as aloof, impartial, and omniscient. It just didn't work for me. I'm a musician; I want to share the music I'm living. As for creating a congenial environment, some students are still my friends and musical associates today. Quite a few have become educators themselves. Music brings people together (even administrators). Clearly, the effort to insert the culture of African and African American people into American education was already underway. There were a lot of people like me going into the profession. We had come up in Black schools in Black neighborhoods immersed in Black culture. We couldn't identify it yet, but the movement was definitely starting.

Until very recently, Black music had always been taught outside of the school, despite its degree of difficulty. Jazz and its evolutions have long excited controversy and criticism at every turn, from Delta blues, New Orleans ragtime, and Afro-Cuban rhythms to swing, mambo, bebop, samba, third stream, free jazz, funk, and hip-hop, among others. It has birthed gospel, R&B, rock, pop, soul, and country music.

If you live and play this tradition long enough, you come to understand just how adaptable this music is to change. It's not accidental that so many folk music traditions all over the world have a common root in jazz and the blues. Hence, the family of this music only gets bigger. It contains multitudes, as Walt Whitman said of himself and his contradictions.

I remember having serious disagreements with Max Roach (one of my idols) about the legitimacy of free improvisation (I was for; he was against). Yet, less than fifteen years later, I saw Max perform riveting duet concerts with Cecil Taylor and Anthony Braxton at Columbia University. Although Max was a polyrhythmic pioneer whose artistry with the drum kit helped invent bebop, he was always searching. That's the spirit of the music. Freedom bound. It gets around. Can't contain it. Ishmael Reed called it Jes Grew in his novel *Mumbo Jumbo*. Watching Max onstage with these younger generation free-jazz maestros, I realized only a living art form could transform itself so rapidly.

# CHAPTER 17

## *Broadway Blues, Barbra Streisand & Sam Rivers*

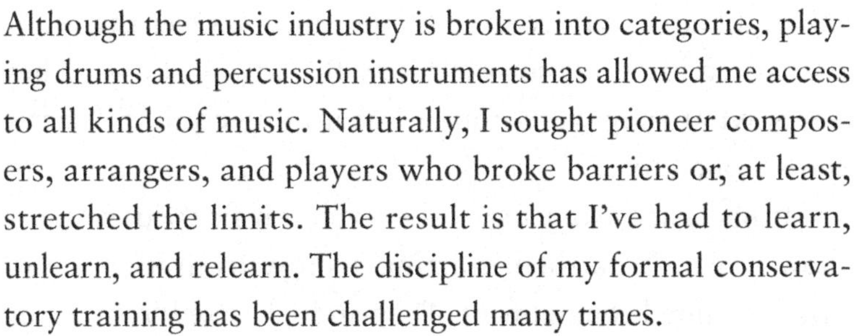

Although the music industry is broken into categories, playing drums and percussion instruments has allowed me access to all kinds of music. Naturally, I sought pioneer composers, arrangers, and players who broke barriers or, at least, stretched the limits. The result is that I've had to learn, unlearn, and relearn. The discipline of my formal conservatory training has been challenged many times.

Once, early in my employment with ABC, while taping a radio show, I had to record a sixteenth-note passage on the xylophone with the reed section, clarinets, and flutes. To put it diplomatically, these cats played the passage with a bit of urgency on the last few notes (they rushed the ending). I played it evenly, as most trained musicians would do. The voice from the control booth said, "Let's do that passage again; it wasn't clean." I may have been right, but I was by myself. Was I going to insist? My sense of survival said: fuck that! So I joined them and rushed those last few notes.

The voice inside the booth said, "That's a take!" Right on!

That experience gave me a fuller understanding of what an accompanist must be sensitive to. The idea is not to be correct but to be in concert with the ensemble. Then the entity is right, and the magic can happen. I was brand new, and these musicians were older and more experienced. I watched them and caught on. I learned to suppress my ego while quietly maintaining my confidence and poise. The most important element is to mesh with the other components so the whole becomes greater than the sum of its parts.

Rapport is everything.

I certainly felt that with *West Side Story*. Robert Griffith and Harold Prince were the producers. Over the years, they often hired me for their new Broadway shows. They knew what they were doing, but no one could predict a show's outcome.

Runs lasted from six weeks (even if it flopped) to more than a year. Back then, starting a show from its point of origin required commitment. The band rehearsed from 9 a.m. to 9 p.m. for two days. On the third day they moved into the theater's orchestra pit and began two weeks of preview shows to fine-tune the production. The director gave notes—corrections, edits, and changes—after each performance to the entire company. Even before these previews on Broadway, shows went on the road first, playing two weeks each in New Haven, Boston, and Philadelphia. Everyone in the show understood nothing was guaranteed except that those opening night reviews determined the show's length.

I was fine with the odds. But after a string of stale, white bread, Broadway shows, I started to weary as the only speck in the buttermilk (I was the only Black musician in the orchestra pit). On the road, it was no problem. Your whole world is just six or seven traveling musicians. You share the same schedule, eat together, and live in the same hotel (at least by the mid-Sixties). You build trust and that feeling of simpatico. But being the only brother in a larger setting can get frisky.

Then, out of nowhere, in 1961, Griffith and Prince offered me *Sail Away* starring Elaine Stritch as Mimi Paragon, with book, music, and lyrics by Noel Coward, who also directed. What a great show to play on. The conductor, Shelly Gold, knew me from my percussion work with the Johnny Richards Orchestra. I fit right in. The play ran for 167 performances.

The next show, however, was so unpleasant that I don't even remember its name. It was the kind of gig you had to sub out occasionally or go mad, but the leader didn't want me to take off at all. Not once. He even tried to chastise me for not tommin'. I was not jovial enough for his liking.

One evening as I climbed the stairs of the orchestra pit, I felt a tension between my eyes. I didn't think about it then, but the pain in my forehead stayed with me. Then Peter Matz called me to do a TV show on ABC. Yeah, buddy! It was two days a week, but one was on a matinee day. Of course, the leader didn't want to give me that one day off. I took a chance and quit on the spot. That night as I climbed those stairs for the last time and stepped out of the theater, I felt the tension in my forehead relax.

It has never come back.

And I've never done a show under those circumstances again.

By contrast, when the chemistry is working, people remember. In 1964, I subbed now and then on *Funny Girl*, a Broadway show starring Barbra Streisand as Fanny Brice. It was her first big break, and she burned the house down night after night. When she quit the show a year later, she called me to play percussion on a national tour. Three years later, she broke into her acting career, winning a Best Actress Oscar for the film version of *Funny Girl*. I watched her skyrocket. That three-octave range—she had it all and the chutzpah to cross borders and break new ground.

A few months later, I got a call. Her limousine driver picked me up and dropped me off at a small airport in New Jersey, where her private jet awaited her and the band. Two seats to an aisle and a private bar. Just six musicians. She used local orchestras in each city. Along for the tour was her husband, actor Elliott Gould.

Show business couples go through many changes, and I felt they had played all the changes in their wedding song. For context, audiences loved Barbra; she was like the Beatles in terms of the level of devotion she elicited from fans. But her Alpha-husband movie star was used to getting a lot more attention. Maybe his jet was in the repair shop, but he was not handling her success so well. Actors have it tough. He couldn't give up the jackass role he had cast himself in.

We arrived in Florida, played a concert to a packed house with a standing ovation, and were chauffeured to a first-class hotel. A tour can become torture and tragedy with missed transportation connections or troubles with the venue or the accommodations. Not with Barbra Streisand. I had never been in a situation that was so luxurious in my life. She knew how to travel. The next day, we were back in her private jet, headed for New Orleans. It was my first time in the city that started it all.

I remember Barbra as a fantastic musician and a model of dependable leadership: always on time, took everything seriously, and it showed. It did not surprise me that she garnered awards for her acting, screenwriting, and directing. Nor that she would succeed in film with such ballsy topics. As for her music, she outgrew the cabaret and show tunes of her early years and crossed over into rock and pop. She kept stretching. She brought that same intensity to her philanthropy work. Like the other greats I have worked with, Barbra always delivered for her audience.

Chemistry goes a long way in music. When Samuel Hawthorne Rivers moved from Boston to New York in 1964, he looked for a drummer who sight read complicated charts. Ken Makanda McIntyre recommended me to him.

Sam lived in a fifth-floor walkup in Harlem on 124th Street, just north of Central Park between Fifth Avenue and

Madison. He had a house full of daughters like I did. His son Sam, Jr., was already a doctor. We rehearsed in his apartment weekly until he made arrangements with a local junior high school that allowed him to use its auditorium in the evenings when the school was empty.

He eventually found a loft space downtown in NoHo (north of Houston Street) on Bond Street. His landlady was Robert DeNiro's mother. Sam and his wife Beatrice opened Studio Rivbea. It became a beacon of the Loft Era, which lasted in New York from the middle Sixties into the late Nineties. For many, especially young people new to the scene, Rivbea was a kind of counter-cultural epicenter. For some, it was the place for free jazz and avant-garde music in downtown Manhattan. Bea served delicious fish sandwiches in this convivial, listener-friendly, do-it-yourself loft space. On any weekend night, there were two bands on the bill: a guest artist and one of three different groups Sam wrote for, played sax in, and led.

I got involved in all three of his bands. In the Sam Rivers Trio, I replaced Norman Conners on drums. Richard Davis played bass, then Cecil McBee, and then Dave Holland. After several years with this configuration, Sam switched out the bass for the tuba, which was played so adeptly by Joseph Daley. We recorded as the Tuba Trio, made three albums at the Bimhuis in Amsterdam, and toured and performed in Europe and across the United States.

With the Sam Rivers Quintet, I doubled on vibraphone and drums. The lineup included Barry Altshul on drums, Dave

Holland on bass, and Ted Dunbar on guitar. We recorded a couple of LPs with Impulse in the early Seventies.

Sam's RivBea Orchestra, with whom I recorded ten different albums, was the largest band I have ever played in. It varied from eighteen pieces at its smallest to thirty-five at its fullest: two basses, two drummers, two pianos, and eight or ten people in each section of saxes, trumpets, and trombones. There are challenges sonically in terms of having that many people hear the definition of a beat together.

The more people you have, the more challenging such basic things can get. Discipline is a bitch, especially in an environment with musicians of different ages and persuasions wisecracking, cutting up, goofing, running around, and whatnot. They're all over the place because that's the way expressive, artistic temperaments go and flow. But Sam was an incredible bandleader. He held the RivBea Orchestra together. Of course, it didn't hurt that he was a hugely talented composer, arranger, alto saxophonist, flutist, bass clarinetist, educator, and jazz elder, whom we all admired and esteemed.

In all three of his groups, the longer we played together, the better we got. That's one reason I enjoy long relationships with the bands I have been in, as well as my ensemble. My association with Sam lasted until he moved with his family to Florida. He left this world in 2011; he was eighty-eight years old.

Ken Makanda McIntyre and Sam Rivers were rare breeds. Each had a unique approach to their instrument. No one else sounded like either one of them. With contemporary composers I had worked with previously (like Partch and Cage), their own performance as instrumentalists was not the focus. Makanda and Sam, however, were masters of their instrument, wrote for the instrument, and led great bands. They were cutting-edge experimentalists, gifted teachers, and remarkable human beings.

While much of their music was composed and required some skill at sight reading, there was free improvisation throughout every performance. The tug between the written and the improvised kept it intriguing. They played a style that was, at times, free of form yet still told a story. Their approaches opened me up conceptually. Each led me to the other and prepared me for the jazz avant-garde music in which I was to become more deeply engaged.

Once again, I was surrounded by inspiring people.

# CHAPTER 18

## *Nat King Cole, Nancy Wilson & Dionne Warwick*

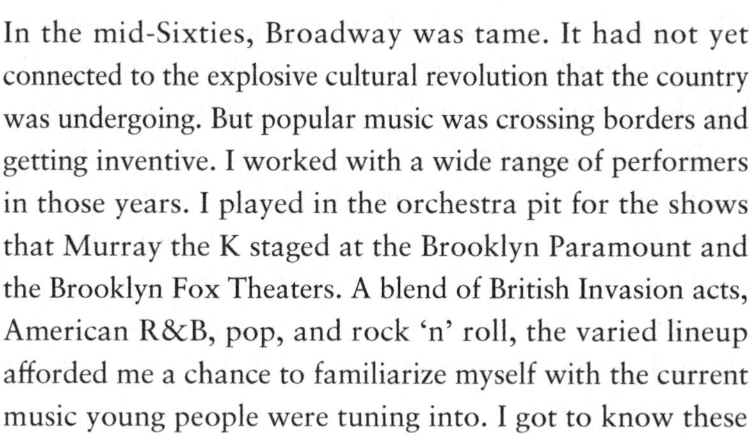

In the mid-Sixties, Broadway was tame. It had not yet connected to the explosive cultural revolution that the country was undergoing. But popular music was crossing borders and getting inventive. I worked with a wide range of performers in those years. I played in the orchestra pit for the shows that Murray the K staged at the Brooklyn Paramount and the Brooklyn Fox Theaters. A blend of British Invasion acts, American R&B, pop, and rock 'n' roll, the varied lineup afforded me a chance to familiarize myself with the current music young people were tuning into. I got to know these white and Black performers for whom I would later play on their record dates.

As for hitting the road with established show business acts, touring with Nat King Cole was a total delight. He had followed the path Belafonte had opened; he made artistic music on TV, film, and in concert that appealed to a mass audience. If Harry gave America ears for the Caribbean, Nat gave America ears for the jazz trio. And what a voice.

Unlike Nina Simone, Nat took things easy. Chicago born (1919), he knew our Uncle Lloyd's sheet music store and played piano at one of the places down the street. With the Cole family band, he made his first record for Decca when he was fifteen. He worked all over Chi-town. The story goes that in this particular (Mafia-owned) club, a drunken audience member insisted that the piano player sing a song. It was an offer Nat couldn't refuse. An amiable cat on or off the stage, Nat knew the lyrics and the changes, and for the first time in public, sang it. People freaked out! They liked it so much that the owner threatened to take away the gig if Nat didn't keep singing. The irony was that he wanted to be famous for his piano playing, and with good reason. He had absorbed the entire tradition and could take it anywhere.

If the public wanted him to sing, he sang so beautifully. But by the time I toured with him, he came off the bandstand, and his voice was hoarse. Even with his throat sore and his health failing, he smoked cigarettes in endless chains. Back then, no one connected cancer with the cancer sticks. He died in 1965, only months after I had last worked and toured with him.

My most vivid memory of Nat was his command of his audience. He got up on the stand, sang "That Rainy Day," and raised his hand upwards. Every face in the place watched his hand stretch out toward the sky. So smooth in the way that he carried himself, his every gesture significant, he mesmerized.

Only two other singers I've worked with could match Nat for that kind of polish and professionalism. The first was Nancy Wilson. Three years younger than me, she hit New York in 1959. I worked in the Apollo Theater's house band. All the big Black theaters had house bands back then. No one had yet heard of Nancy. This was her first gig in New York. She came out and sang "Save Your Love for Me." We all left the Apollo singing that song. It became an R&B classic.

Cannonball Adderley had been the guy who told her to get to the Big Apple, and she recorded it with his group. Their album, Nancy Wilson and Cannonball Adderley, is one of the finest examples of jazz ballads, with the singer and the band so attuned to each other. Within four weeks of her Big Apple arrival, the Blue Morocco booked Nancy, and she hit big. Up ahead, she would forge a great body of work as a song stylist in multiple genres. She would cross a few borders as a TV and film actress, achieve worldwide acclaim, and be celebrated with every jazz honor and civil rights accolade.

The only other singer with that degree of voice mastery and superb delivery was the divine Sarah Vaughan. I remember my first record date with her. She came into the studio with her head wrapped up, not looking like the glamorous Sassy at all. But when she stepped up to the microphone, her voice came out like a healing force: sweet, precise, heaven-sent.

Like Nat, Aretha Franklin, and Carmen McRae, Sarah was one of those excellent piano players who could accompany themselves, even though promoters preferred them out front, alone at the microphone. I worked with Carmen on a couple of recordings and did a tour where she was one of the acts. She delivered that kind of polish every time. So did Aretha but in her own way.

As for Dionne Warwick, I got to know her through working for her sister Delaia Juanita, known as Dee Dee, who was the director of the Garden State Choir. She hired me to play (and then taught me) gospel tambourine, which led me to hundreds of record dates just playing tambourine. Dee Dee, Dionne, and their aunt, Cissy Houston, then formed the Gospelaires, a gospel-singing trio managed by their mother, Lee Drinkard. They played with the Drinkard Sisters (Dionne was in this group, too), which led to Dionne singing backup for the Drifters. That's when she came to the attention of songwriter Burt Bacharach and his lyricist Hal David. She debuted as a soloist in 1962 and turned their "Don't Make Me Over" into a hit, the first of many brilliant collaborations with Bachrach and David throughout the decade. I played on her TV shows, concerts, and tours. Like Nancy Wilson and Barbra Streisand, Dionne pioneered new ground beyond singing. She entered the acting profession, became a TV host, and a goodwill ambassador for the United Nations.

Each of these singers has a distinctive, identifying sound that has gained access to my emotional life over the years. Their vocal performance starts with a good groove; the rhythm's really popping, and the horns are playing something easy, not necessarily fast or volatile, just moving along and touching me, opening the way for the vocalist. I'm ready to be transported at the sound of her voice in that first chorus. That's what I'm after.

By the mid-Sixties, Mary and I were raising four young and beautiful daughters. Lynn (born in 1958), Leslie (born in 1961), and Mikey (born in 1963) had all been delivered at Columbia Presbyterian Hospital in New York. Stephanie (born in 1965) had been delivered at Mercy Hospital in Long Island after we left our five-year run in Brooklyn and moved to Hempstead in 1963. We stayed until 1985. Mary taught at Grand Avenue Elementary School in nearby Baldwin for a time.

I was surrounded by inspiring people at home.

# CHAPTER 19

## *Motown, Aretha Franklin, Joe Zawinul & Van Morrison*

From the mid-Sixties to the early Seventies, I worked my ass off in the recording studio. I averaged two sessions a day; sometimes I made five dates in one day.

The big change came in 1967 when three things shifted my focus of attention professionally: I quit substitute teaching for the Board of Ed; the ABC studio orchestra gig ended (relocated to Los Angeles); and I subbed out the music classes I had been teaching for seven years at the Third Street Settlement to percussionist and friend Omar Clay.

Among other right place/right time encounters as a drummer and percussionist in these years, I had become part of a killin' rhythm section with bassist Chuck Rainey and guitarists Cornell Dupree and Eric Gale. We worked in tandem with composer-arranger-band-leader Sy Oliver and composer-arranger-record producer-conductor Horace Ott.

All these people turned out to be historic, especially in delivering jazz and R&B flavors to the popular music of the era. And those early years building a network in Philly, Chicago, and Detroit through recording demos were now paying off as well. I played drums on all the Gladys Knight and the Pips 45 hit singles and on *United*, the only collaborative album done by Marvin Gaye and Tammy Terrell.

Another (occasional) addition to the rhythm section was funk drummer Bernard Purdie. Known for the Purdie Shuffle—triplets against a half-time backbeat—"Pretty" Purdie was the drummer for Aretha Franklin and her opening act, King Curtis and the Kingpins. That's King Curtis playing sax on Ms. Franklin's records. He was her musical director. As for his band, I loved playing with the Kingpins. We really brought the funk.

Playing vibraphone and percussion, I recorded, toured, and did live TV shows with Aretha Franklin from 1965 to 1978, including her amazing performance at the 1971 Montreux Jazz Festival in Switzerland. Aretha Franklin forged her own way with a voice that always reached me on the deepest level. Every time.

She grew up singing gospel and switched to singing jazz standards, but once she started working with Atlantic

Records, she found her sound. Soul music. Like Motown, James Brown, Sly Stone, and Jimi Hendrix, Black musical acts were stepping out of the chitlin circuit and crossing over to larger audiences and bigger venues. But no one had it goin' on like Ms. Franklin.

The strength of her voice moved the unmovable. She was quite a performer. Maybe it was her beginnings playing the gospel circuit, but she really got into the spirit of the music. I remember she hit a high note on one tune and started jumping with the beat. While she was at mid-jump, one of her breasts came out of her gown but magically returned to its place underneath her dress by the next jump. I don't think she even noticed.

In the studio, she came in and sang and played the piano. And Eric, Cornell, Chuck, Bernie, and I played with her. Producers let her do what she was going to do, and then they wrote out the lead sheets. We fit the rhythm section around her. We caught all the little riffs and things she did and matched them. The producers then took that back into the studio and got the backup singers to come in and arrange their parts around that. Then they added the strings and mixed it all together.

But we did it in a compartmental fashion. They might overdub Aretha's solo if they didn't like what she had done originally, but a lot of the stuff she did originally fit so well because it was so integrated with her piano playing and everything else.

So many fond memories are embedded in the songs of hers we played. Once, years after working with her, I walked a street in Paris and heard her cover of Otis Redding's "Respect" blasting out of a window. I stopped, sat, and heard the record to its end. I had to smile. It felt like a message from the Queen of Soul that she was still around, still gettin' her props.

Playing vibes on her Lady Soul LP that Atlantic produced in 1968 was another career highlight. I think it's highly ranked among all-time favorite albums because the band, her vocals, and the material really came together. Everything was just right for that session. The personnel included Spooner Oldham, Bobby Womack, Eric Clapton, Frank Wess, and King Curtis, among others, with Cissy Houston and Aretha's sister Carolyn on backup vocals.

Arthea Franklin left an indelible mark on the music. Like the other pioneers I have worked with, she crossed borders and genres and still made the song hers. I send doubters to the internet to hear her soulful "Nessun Dorma" performance at the 1998 Grammy Awards.

In that same year of 1968, I played percussion on Joe Zawinul's *The Rise and Fall of the Third Stream.* It was an adventurous blend of jazz and classical music with cellos, violas, sax, trumpet, and a rhythm section. Two years older than me, Joe was the ultimate "No Guts, No Glory, Welcome to New York" story. Born and raised in Vienna, he was conservatory-trained and a staff pianist for Polydor in Austria throughout the 1950s. He had chops; he played with everyone over there. But when he hit the States in 1959, he felt intimidated by superstar jazz musicians in the Apple. He hadn't stretched into the musical pioneer he would eventually become.

He got a job as the pianist at Minton's. Dinah Washington was at the bar one night, and so was I. Dinah was just being herself—that is to say funny, raucous, outrageous, and strongly opinionated. When she didn't like the comping, she asked, "Who's that playing piano?" Folks said it was Joe, but that did not stop her. She walked over, put her hand on his shoulder, and made him get up. She sat and started playing with the band.

I doubt any of us would have put another musician on the spot like that, no matter who they were. But Dinah took him to school. Joe joined Dinah's band shortly after that. His tenure with her led to his playing with Cannonball Adderley's group. Joe next worked with Miles Davis and helped invent fusion, a blending of jazz and rock music. Joe then formed Weather Report with Wayne Shorter, a band that took fusion even further.

Joe Zawinul was one of many musicians crossing musical borders. Between 1967 and 1969, I recorded with jazz trombonist Kai Winding (Penny Lane and Time), two albums with the psychedelic band Pearls Before Swine (as a guest artist), the electronic avant-garde *Rock and Other Four Letter Words*, Phil Upchurch's soul jazz *Feeling Blue*, Tamiko Jones' jazz-funk-soul *I'll Be Anything For You*, bluegrass virtuosos Peter Rowan and David Grisman's psychedelic rock *Earth Opera*, multireedist Rahsaan Roland Kirk's *Left and Right*, Jerome Richardson's jazz versions of pop hits on *Groove Merchant*, and Solomon Burke's R&B album *King Solo-*

*mon*, among others. One of my most fulfilling experiences in the recording studio was *Brer Soul*, an LP written by my doo-wop singing homie Melvin Van Peebles. I arranged all the songs, conducted the band, and played drums and percussion. We followed that up with *Ain't Supposed to Die a Natural Dea*th in 1971.

There were recording dates with country music, samba, easy listening, gospel, folk, and folk-rock. And then there was The Fugs. I performed with them in clubs, wrote music, arranged strings, and played on *Tenderness Junction*, *It Crawled into My Hand*, *Honest* and *Golden Filth*. Ed Sanders, Tuli Kupferberg, and those guys were a lot of fun. They had a madcap, anarchist spirit. Whenever we were hanging out and politics came up, much to my amusement, I found out that we were on the same wavelength. Turns out we all wrote poetry as well.

But nothing is more reminiscent of the era's musical border-crossing than the session for Van Morrison's *Astral Weeks*. I remember getting a call in September'68 from bassist Richard Davis, who was putting the musicians together. Richard and I had been bandmates in Sam Rivers' trio. He asked me to play vibraphone and percussion. The band included Connie Kay, drummer for the Modern Jazz Quartet, guitarist Jay Berliner (from Mingus' band), and John Payne on flute and soprano sax, the only one of us who had played with Van. We didn't know him or his music.

I know it is an important record and considered one of the best pop albums in history, but there was next to no preparation. We had chord changes; we didn't need much else. Van stepped out of his booth, sat in the big room with us, and played all the tunes. He returned to his booth as shyly as he had come out; we rolled tape. Although the album has received much praise for the arrangements, over the three sessions, we improvised the whole thing on the spot from the structure of the tunes. Richard had a feel for what the Belfast singer-songwriter was up to, and we just followed Richard's lead. Warner Brothers, the record company, added the string quartet later at another session. Critics have also been confounded by how to classify the LP, but Van struck me as a blues singer. That's why it was such a good fit.

From my earliest days in music, I have had the opportunity to be in the right place at the right time with the right skills. Doubling as a drummer and a percussionist, I had a distinct advantage, especially when experimentation and something new was involved, whether touring or recording.

Not every jazz musician, composer, and leader made the change. Some explored musical ideas that were not popular yet or might never be. Following one's own drumbeat is what defines a jazz artist. But the late Sixties was also a time for a change in thinking, particularly among many Black musicians.

The mainstreaming of African American culture via novels, poetry, activism, films, TV, radio, tours, and records, especially in response to civil and human rights issues, challenged the status quo. Our music, previously marketed as "race records," put Black pop, soul, funk, jazz, R&B, and rock into the homes of millions of non-Black people.

This advancement brought success as well as the formation of new strategies. A discontent many decades in the making was now interrogating the industry's plantation model. The branding and the name game imposed on our music harmed us. Musicians, particularly those who were also educators, understood that the word jazz belittled the music and kept it from being taken seriously by university music programs and commercial venues.

The term jazz presumed incorrectly that nothing "classical" was going on, just riffing and jiving, nothing written or arranged, nothing requiring virtuosic skill. Hence, low art.

It may have started as the music played in New Orleans' Storyville district's brothels ("jazz houses"), but before it traveled up the Mississippi to Chicago and beyond, it grew by leaps and bounds. Like Buddy Bolden before him, Louis Armstrong synthesized all the previous trumpet-cornet styles into his own, taking the music into a classical dimension via his virtuosity. The same might be said of pianist and composer Jelly Roll Morton, another Crescent City native. In fact, a study of each instrument and who played it from then to now reveals how much virtuosity and high art the tradition embodies.

In truth, the music has little to do with the sex trade and everything to do with the Black experience in America. We are central to its invention, interpretation, and mutation. Its truer name is African American classical music. Along with respect via naming things properly, Black composers, arrangers, and musicians were tired of our stuff getting stolen.

How were other people making more money with our music than we were?

In short, like every generation before us, we were intent on owning, producing, and distributing our music. While some of us got increased exposure and opportunity to advance as individuals, we also brought our talents and resources together, epitomized by the Loft Era that was coming into prominence. Our musical projects were no longer limited to the world of record companies, contractors, and promoters. We wanted to present our music to our audiences in our way.

It was the next step in a journey of ten thousand steps.

# CHAPTER 20

## *The Loft Era, Studio WIS & the Avant-Garde*

Nothing stays the same for long in New York City.

In the mid-1940s, the small clubs that dotted 52nd Street had made it a world-famous address for the bebop revolution. But by 1967, the street was lost to the developers. Call it urban renewal or creative destruction, but it felt more like gentrification. Rarely did the program do any good for the people and the culture it displaced.

On 52nd Street, some clubs relocated; most went under. All were torn down. So befell the fate of the building that housed the rehearsal/performance space off 10th Avenue that I started with Perk and Jack in 1961. Six years later, the west side neighborhood got the John Jay College of Criminal Justice and a new wing of Roosevelt Hospital, and we got put on the street.

I miraculously found another space, a loft at 151 West 21st Street, and we moved in seamlessly. We called it Chelsea Performing Space Studio WIS. It was roomy and an ideal location: equidistant from Harlem and Brooklyn, with easy subway access and free parking. I took over the lease from Peter Berry, a friend and percussionist. Rent was a whopping $95 a month.

Left over from the earlier days of the garment industry, these floor-through empty loft spaces had been converted by artists into living/working studios since the early 1950s. Rent was cheap as the properties were mostly abandoned or neglected. We certainly weren't the only ones turning lofts into studios. Though we had been among the first in '61, by '67, the loft era in the New York art and music scene was going full strength. Sam Rivers' Studio Rivbea, trumpeter James DuBois' Studio We, saxophonist Claude Lawrence's studio on Lower Broadway, and drummer Rashied Ali's Ali's Alley stand out in my memory.

We had our unique program, but almost every loft that offered concerts also offered kids musical training and educational programs. We were advancing the music, introducing it to the next generation, and creating opportunities for young composers and players. We offered band rehearsal space and a place for composers to write music. We invited audiences into our studios regularly and produced concerts that we recorded.

Although Mayor John Lindsay famously called New York "Fun City" at this time, rents went up, and work in the music business was not always easy for a newcomer to find. I offered some young cats a place to learn—and sometimes sleep. Chicago-born guitarist Jean-Paul Bourelly made Studio WIS his home for eleven months. He heard everyone at our studio, absorbing a range of music from solo performances by Cecil Taylor to straight-ahead jazz with big band arrangements. Looking back, I can see so clearly that the real inspiration behind Studio WIS was Pops. Our loft was an extension of what my father was doing in our apartment on the South Side.

"Warren is more than just a cousin and family member to me. He is a mentor, friend, and father figure as well. My dad, Warren, and his brother Frank were compadres growing up; many people, including myself, consider Warren and Frank my uncles. Warren took my brother and me in when we were trying to finish our final years of high school, and my dad had to move out of New York for a job in Pennsylvania. He also allowed me to stay at his New York City loft after graduating college. During these periods, I gained so much knowledge and perspective about being a jazz musician and a human being. Aside from being a roadie for his gigs, he allowed me to perform in his loft and connected me to some important members of the jazz community, including Max Roach, whom I talked with on a couple of occasions." —*Dr. William E. Smith, Associate Professor of Music Technology, Bowie State University.*

New York in the late Sixties was a fertile period for crossing borders. Musicians became more experimental. For example, around this time, I started working with free jazz trumpeter Bill Dixon at Judson Church in Greenwich Village. He was a great collaborator. With Judith Dunn, Bill formed a jazz-dance company. With Mike Mantler and Carla Bley, Bill created Jazz Composers Guild to promote orchestral avant-garde music.

Another feature of exploring less commercially driven music was the phenomenon of single-instrument family ensembles taking shape. Probably the first was Howard Johnson's Substructure, a group of virtuoso tuba players (later known as Gravity) who possess extraordinary improvisational skills. Then the Baritone Sax Retinue emerged, led by Hamiet Bluiett, Charles Davis, and Mario Rivera. Brass Proud, an ensemble of trumpeters, showed up next; Bill Lee (Spike's dad) ran the Bass Violin Choir; and of course, there was M'Boom, Max Roach's marvelous percussion ensemble.

At Studio WIS, we grew a reputation for innovative percussion programs as well as Composer's Workshop Ensemble concerts and avant-garde jazz performances. My partner Anton Reid and I produced a series of percussion concerts. I led a children's percussion workshop that lasted many years, serving kids in the neighborhood from the ages of two to seven years old.

Charlie Persip and I did a series of master classes for professional drummers and university students. We videotaped many lecture series and over two thousand performances.

For my ensemble, I wrote original arrangements of material that I adapted from composers I liked, as well as my original compositions. All these pieces called for improvisation. The repertoire grew to over three hundred works. Looking back, I was glad to have recorded and archived it.

As for the avant-garde, Studio WIS became a meeting ground for musicians and composers out of the Midwest and down from New England. It was the first stop in New York for many members of the Association for the Advancement of Creative Musicians (AACM) out of Chicago and members of the Black Artists Group (BAG) out of St Louis. Ethnomusicologist Bill Cole taught at Dartmouth and came by to pick up on what we were doing. Word spread.

By 1996 Studio WIS was probably the last loft space to exist. It was a great run. As musicians and lovers of this music, we achieved a truly communitarian spirit. We didn't seek to replace the musical status quo; we wanted to create an alternative and succeeded.

Despite our longevity, I came to see a familiar pattern take place. The artist-as-pioneer class showed up for the cheap rents and helped the poverty-stricken neighborhood rise out of hard times. As these edgy locales grew arty, an informal network developed. Artists began exhibiting visual art and performing in dance, music, poetry, and drama recitals in their living or working spaces. Soho, Chelsea, the Lower East Side, Greenwich Village, and Harlem attracted devoted local supporters and international tourists. Money moved, which caused the attention of developers who promptly built luxury condominiums no artist could afford to live in.

Although this grassroots loft scene thrived for thirty years, we know how this story ends: lots of people benefitted, but there was no substantial support from neighborhood, borough, city, state, or nation. The spaces were self-financed and sustained personally by individual artists. A more New York way of describing it is that Manhattan is a small island ruled by a predatory real estate market. By the mid-1990s, there were no empty or unoccupied spaces left.

From my first days at Studio WIS, I sensed we were onto something historic. We ran, scheduled, improved, composed, arranged, rehearsed and recorded our music there. We printed flyers (which I saved copies of for archival purposes). We provided a meeting place for ideas, musicians, and performances, and rehearsal space for the bands of Max Roach, Sun Ra, Abdullah Ibrahim (Dollar Brand), and many more.

Thanks to the other musicians and composers who opened loft spaces during this period, we achieved something substantial through cooperation and the right intention. There was a powerful feeling of community. We had juice! When George Wein of the Newport Jazz Festival and other jazz promoters ignored us, we put together the New York Musicians Festival in 1972. It was a hit. The second year it took place, we made sure to attract the European press because they also covered Newport. In our third year, we were even stronger. Wein got frightened. To say it more diplomatically, he got interested in what we were doing and offered us space in Newport.

Any surviving participants of the era will testify that this was a golden age for creative musicians and the whole movement of contemporary music. It opened opportunities to perform in major concert halls in and around New York City. It even inspired the initiative to create the Jazz at Lincoln Center program.

One of the most fortunate things about Studio WIS was a piano for composers. In the late Sixties into the early Seventies, Gil Evans dropped by often. He liked to compose through the night at Studio WIS; it was just a short walk up from his apartment. I often closed the place and drove back to Long Island when he appeared. His children were young and not yet into his music, though they dove in when they got older.

Through Studio WIS, I got to know him on a whole other level.

# PART 3

*Touring the World, 1969-2022*

# CHAPTER 21

## *Duke Ellington, Charles Mingus & Gil Evans*

My three favorite composers are Duke Ellington, Charles Mingus, and Gil Evans.

As a bandleader, Duke provided me with one of the most inspiring experiences of my life. I was on tour with Nat King Cole, and in the lobby of my hotel in Boston, I noticed the entrance in the lower lobby of a nightclub called Storyville. When I returned later, I saw a group of people downstairs and checked it out. On the way, I recognized Russell Procope and Jimmy Hamilton. It was Duke's band! I told them I was with the show next door. They invited me into the club.

"We're getting ready to rehearse. Would you like to come in and check it out?"

What an opportunity!

Duke hadn't arrived yet. All the cats stood around the bar, smoking, drinking, never thinking of rehearsal, nonchalant. Then Duke entered and sat at the piano, got comfortable, and started playing a nice easy blues. Bassist Ernie Shepherd reacted first, put down his drink, and had his bass out of its cover before Duke finished his first chorus.

When Ernie started, my idol Sam Woodyard, sharp as a switchblade, looked up. He held his cigarette and drink in his left hand while gesturing to make his point with the mighty right. I still can't do that! As soon as Sam heard that bass line underneath Duke's piano, he broke off immediately, got right up there, and started laying down that impeccable time, and the shit was on now!

Everyone was focused on getting up there to get a piece of this groove. A sweet trumpet solo was followed by a clarinet chorus or three. Then I noticed a lone figure, his tenor out, come striding across the stage. Paul Gonsalves, the last to arrive, was ready to hit the downbeat at the top of the next chorus. But the downbeat never came. Right on the one, Duke stood and cut the band off with an emphatic sweep of his right hand. Absolute silence swept the room, and Ellington said in a mellow tone, "Now, gentlemen, let's look at the passage we kind of fumbled through last evening."

How elegant, how cool could a bandleader possibly be! It was a lesson in psychology as well as musicianship and discipline. After the show that night, I got back in time to catch most of the last set. The effect of the rehearsal was evident in the performance. One of the trumpet players played a rhythm on the cowbell I had heard in the rehearsal, but this time others picked up claves and maracas in the section and transported the audience to a Caribbean isle. The band swung right on through as usual and left us dancing out of the club and into the night.

As goes my first nickname (from the Ellington tune "Moonglow"), Duke's music was in my bloodstream prenatally. I've followed that band through the decades. In a lucky twist of fate, I got to play drums with the Mercer Ellington-led band every Monday night for seven years in the 1990s. I fit right into their scene.

To my Duke-drunk ear, Charles Mingus absorbed many of Ellington's compositional strengths. Their songs are so well made. In addition, Mingus made art in the here and now, weaving into his emotionally explosive music a taste of poetry, politics, humor, prayer meetings, and other elements of Black culture.

Before I signed on with Mingus, I knew that he had a temper and a troubled mind. When I read his autobiography *Beneath the Underdog* years later, I got a better sense of what he was going through. I admired Mingus. He got testy around musicians who were less committed to their art than he was. I understood the value of immersion in the music— that's how I had grown up.

As for the stories about Mingus being demanding, I was confident because I had the training and experience to play anything he asked of me. As a percussionist, I was somewhat unique due to my familiarity with the jazz tradition. Back then, most classically trained percussionists were not interested in improvisation or respectful of it. But composers like Mingus and Gil Evans (and arrangers like Johnny Richards, Eddie Sauter, and Bill Finnegan) expanded their visions of what jazz and improvisation could do inside larger ensembles. I played as a percussionist on some of Mingus' compositions for orchestra, in concerts, and on a few recordings. The Town Hall concert in 1962 was such an occasion; Mingus performed a composition for a full orchestra. We had several rehearsals before the concert. The performance was filmed, though I didn't view it until many years later, and I was surprised to see myself playing timpani and percussion. Mingus always remembered me after that concert. I continued to pull good things out of his music these many years later.

Likewise, Gil Evans. As a composer, he opened the music up in so many ways. His collaborations with Miles Davis, especially in symphonic settings, really took it to another level. Like Duke and Mingus, Gil was a master orchestrator with an uncanny feel for harmonic combinations, especially in a large ensemble. Gil often had brilliant jazz musicians playing traditional symphonic instruments—French horn, for example—to a jazz arrangement. I fit right into his scene.

Astrology alert: Duke, Mingus, Gil, and I were born under the sun sign. Taurus. One could call us mule-stubborn or grounded. I prefer the latter term because these three composers showed me how to build a melody around an orchestra from the ground up. Those ethereal voicings and depth of feeling they achieve are possible because of the solid foundation they provide. Playing and listening to their music has been highly inspirational in my composing and arranging.

It started with Gil around '62 or '63. I did a job with the Johnny Richards Jazz Orchestra that ended early. We all hit Birdland to catch Gil Evans and his group.

Somehow the night before, Gil's guitar player Chuck Wayne got into a fistfight with drummer Philly Joe Jones on the bandstand. They were so drunk and rowdy that Gil fired them. He was on the search for a drummer and a guitar player when we walked in. One of the cats in the Johnny Richards band told Gil I could sight read well. So I sat in on the drum kit. Gil remembered.

In 1967, he formed an experimental orchestra. Howard Johnson, my old friend and a great tuba and baritone sax player, called me about playing percussion (and sometimes drums) in this new ensemble. I was all for it.

The minute I saw Gil at the rehearsal, I told him I wanted to study music with him.

"I ain't no teacher," he told me.

My heart sank.

Then he added, "Why don't you write somethin' for the band?"

So I started writing music for the Gil Evans Orchestra. I became the percussionist. Sunny Murray was on the drum kit, but Gil was the only musician in the band who could deal with Sunny's concept. So, over time, I became the drummer.

About a year or two after that, Gil called me at midnight and asked me to write a love song for a film score due tomorrow. The next morning, I sent him "Love in the Open." We recorded it that day. That's how Gil liked to do things. The tune is on *Blues in Orbit*; it became a standard in the band's repertoire. Much of the stuff I wrote to help him became part of the band literature.

When it came to big band music, Gil had a great way of working. He wrote some chord changes on a few bars, and then it went up a half step and came down a whole step before returning to the original. He left these sketches at the piano, and the next day a team of us came in and filled out the whole thing. We went into the studio and recorded it just like that. It was the ultimate apprenticeship with the maestro.

I loved playing in his big band. He was democratic when it came to arrangements he liked. He used several of my charts on *The Gil Evans Orchestra Plays the Music of Jimi Hendrix*, an LP. I played chimes, percussion, and vibraphone. Although scheduled to play the recording date, Hendrix died in September of 1970, just a few weeks before. That would have been quite a coming together of guitar virtuosity and ensemble playing.

I played percussion on *The Gil Evans Orchestra, Montreux Jazz Festival 1974*, and *There Comes a Time*. Touring Europe with his ensemble was another career high point. I learned a great deal in my twenty years with Gil.

I also worked with George Russell and his big band during these years. Playing drums on his *New York Big Band* LP in 1982 was another rare experience. All these pioneers—Gil Evans, Miles Davis, John Coltrane, Bill Evans, Eric Dolphy, and Art Farmer, among others—had George

Russell and his Lydian Chromatic Concept of Tonal Organization to thank for their inquiries into modal music. George had written the escape plan out of a narrow musical frame and into freer improvisational possibilities.

George and Gil experimented with big band post-bop music and took jazz composition to a new level by incorporating symphonic elements. And it swung so beautifully. These associations with two of my hero composers gave me an invaluable opportunity to study their concepts and absorb the music from inside the orchestra. No other circumstance could have afforded me this insight.

But Gil Evans did me an extraordinary favor that I've yet to mention—one that led to the first of many musical tours out of the country.

# CHAPTER 22

## *Musical Director, Janis Joplin & Europe Tour*

One day in the fall of 1968, I just happened to be standing next to Gil Evans after a rehearsal when a tall, bespectacled, long-haired cat named Albert Grossman entered the studio. He was the manager of Bob Dylan, Joan Baez, and Peter, Paul and Mary.

Grossman had taste; his first client had been Odetta. And Grossman had moxie; he created the Newport Folk Festival to highlight Odetta's talent.

"I'm managing a young blues singer and need a musical director," Grossman said. Gil wasn't interested. But Gil had taste; he had moxie, too.

"Why don't you ask this guy here?" Gil said and pointed at me.

"You?" Grossman said.

"Yes, of course, me," I said with all the taste and moxie I could muster.

So Albert Grossman hired me on the spot to be Janis Joplin's musical director. I didn't know who Janis was then, but I signed on because I liked the idea of a European tour and a stay in San Francisco.

The next day, the record company flew me out to San Francisco, where the group was performing at the Winter Garden. It was an ice hockey arena—an acoustical disaster. The first thing I noticed was the volume level. On the plane, I had purchased two miniature bottles of wine and saved the corks for protection. I needed it.

The company delivered a new, state-of-the-art Tanberg four-track, reel-to-reel tape recorder. I taped two shows, returned to the hotel, and began transcribing the music. Their performances had been built around jamming, the results varying from show to show. Said kindly, it was hit and miss.

Two weeks later, I handed the group my arrangements of their songs. I was able to refine the structure in a consistent format. I wrote out parts and structured each song so that the presentation was consistent from performance to performance. I recorded and wrote out each part so that we could rehearse each song.

We began a week of rehearsals. I managed to get them to listen to each other more, turn down the volume on their electric instruments and pay closer attention to dynamics.

We had an *Ed Sullivan Show* performance scheduled at the end of the year, so there was plenty of motivation, preparation, and focus. And it showed. They played well.

Then there was the tour, which began in the early spring of 1969. The first stop was at the Royal Albert Hall in London.

The Rolling Stones loaned us their studio for rehearsals. It was a rather funky basement place and not very clean, but it served the purpose. When a journalist asked Mick Jagger if he was going to the show, he refused to attend because Janis wasn't Black! Can you believe that shit? Actually, he phrased it: "If I want to go see a Black American singer, I'll go see a Black American singer!"

Janis was sensitive, and that hurt her feelings. I won't go into the irony of it because it's too obvious not to laugh. Nevertheless, nothing stopped Janis. A force of nature, she turned it out at every performance. She had boundless energy in her singing, and the audiences felt her. A bit bashful at times, she was prone to feeling insecure about following a hot opening act. That might last until she hit the stage. Then she was the boss.

I had to hand it to this performer. She lived the blues and knew the secret of the blues: the more she moaned and groaned, wept and wailed, pleaded and prayed, the better the audience felt. She was in the tradition. She brought the medicine. One of her biggest influences was Bessie Smith, who got her start singing at Uncle Lloyd's sheet music store. When I learned that Janis had paid for Bessie Smith's headstone, which read "The Greatest Blues Singer in the World

Will Never Stop Singing, Bessie Smith, 1895-1937" in 1970, it did not surprise me.

Generosity and respect for the blues tradition were Janis' style.

How was this for a full circle: I finally got to Europe, like my father before me. But instead of carrying Uncle Lloyd's charts in my suitcase like Pops, I had written the charts for these Haight-Ashbury musicians who were playing music that pre-dated their lives, music that Bessie Smith had first delivered to the world in Uncle Lloyd's music store.

Janis' group, the Kozmic Blues Band, was something else. The rhythm section was Keyboardist Stephen Ryder, drummer Roy Markowitz, and bassist Brad Campbell. Cornelius "Snooky" Flowers was the baritone saxman. He and Sam Houston Andrew, the guitarist (left over from Big Brother and the Holding Company, her earlier band), handled the background singing. Snooky referred to Janis as "the baddest bitch on the planet!" Janis loved that, and she deserved the compliment.

On the first day in London, as soon as I checked into my room, I looked outside and saw a town square with a lot of people milling around. I got right out there immediately.

Soon I heard someone say to me, "Hey brother, where you from?"

Two brothers with West Indian accents introduced themselves. They lived in Nottinghill Gate. One of them was a doctor.

The next question was: "Do you smoke?"

On my affirmative, we went to a nearby pub for a McKesson, my first Stout. And from there, we went up to my room.

The brothers rolled up a blunt mixed with tobacco, which was how they did it in Europe then. Well, after a couple of passes, I was just about fucked up. I had to sit down; then I had to lie down. I started laughing. I wasn't completely out, but I was helpless. And I thought, "I don't know these cats. They could rob me, take all my shit, and I'd just have to lie here and laugh at them and myself." Well, the brothers were righteous. They covered me up and left, then called back about a half hour later to make sure I was all right.

After London, we continued to hit great audiences: Rome, Paris, Copenhagen, and Amsterdam. These were great cities to sightsee and photograph, two of my favorite things. As for being social with the band, I liked them well enough, but I was thirty-five years old. The environment was a bit on the young twenty side. I mostly hung with the drummer, Roy, who had studied with me in New York a few years earlier. He loved accompanying me to the jazz clubs. It was such a treat to hear. I'd get a chance to sit in occasionally, which kept me feeling connected. And I saw a lot of old friends, like J.C. Moses and Ed Thigpen, who lived in Europe.

After that tour of eight weeks, though, I'd had enough of rock-style blues for a while. I had given that band all that I could for eighteen months. I recorded several of the tour performances as well as the gig in San Francisco. They continued to use my arrangements long after I stepped off.

The job paid fairly well. But there was a limit to my influence. When I told my father I had quit, he said, "Son, don't you think you could have just hung in there long enough to save for a nest egg?"

I put the earphones on his ears.

He listened for about two minutes, took off the earphones, shook his head and never mentioned it again.

As with Nat King Cole, Janis Joplin died within a year of my working with her. The difference was that Nat had been an international star for over twenty years, but Janis was only getting started. Her biggest-selling album, *Pearl*, was released posthumously. It contained her biggest-selling single, "Me and Bobby McGee."

# CHAPTER 23

## *The Negro Ensemble Company & Family in Paris*

I wasn't home from Janis Joplin's tour a week before I was off again to Europe, this time with the Negro Ensemble Company. We played London, Paris, and Rome.

A theater collective led by Douglas Turner Ward that produced innovative Black theater talent—actors, directors, writers, and producers—the NEC were cultural vanguards but far from being the first such organization. Every city in the USA had a predominantly African American neighborhood, especially with the great northern migration up from the South, post-slavery and Civil War. Each neighborhood had its own cultural definition that was made up of churches, schools, and meeting places, which provided young singers, musicians, actors, directors, set designers, and playwrights with the opportunity to grow their skills. The result is that the African influence upon American culture is far more obvious than the European culture—and more obvious in the fine arts and performing arts.

The NEC was not born in a convent. They had produced Lorraine Hansberry's *A Raisin in the Sun* and Amiri Baraka's *Dutchmen*. In other words, they didn't shy away from playwrights telling it like it is. They had a pioneering spirit. But we were touring with its most controversial play, *The Song of the Lusitanian Bogey*. Written by Peter Weiss, a Swiss native, the play focuses on the exploitation of African forced labor in the diamond mines of South Africa and Rhodesia. That turned out to be a touchy subject. My longtime friend, Perk, composed and conducted the music.

In our first week, during one performance in London, a young conservative radical stood in front of the mezzanine and shouted, "The Rhodesians are our allies! The Rhodesians are our allies!" He threw a handful of printed leaflets over the balcony into the orchestra seats. We saw all this clearly on stage, but we ignored the disturbance and continued, on script. While we played, we watched Perk, our conductor, burst through the balcony door as the protester approached the exit. No one laughed (until later) as Perk physically engaged the rebel. They collided at the top of the stairs. Like two pencils wound up in a rubber band, they tumbled down the middle aisle, stopped only from falling over into the audience below by the railing. Perk escorted the pamphleteer up the stairs and out of the theater. No one in the orchestra section of the audience saw this, but those of us playing and acting onstage saw the whole thing go down. As Oscar Brown, Jr. said, "But I was cool!" We all were.

After the show that night, I paid a visit to a couple I had met while on the Janis tour. Rhoden, an English-style Black Panther, and his beautiful blond wife Nora, an importer of South African jewelry and artifacts, lived in Nottinghill Gate. They had a hip record collection, and Rhoden loved to discuss civil rights for Blacks on both sides of the Atlantic. I knew I would look these folks up if I was ever back in London.

I visited them more for comfort than to elicit their reactions. I told them, "Our own conductor had to 'escort' that fool out of the place! Here we are, a Black American theater company on the road, sending an important message about white exploitation of Blacks in Mother Africa. With a small minority of whites integrated throughout the company, we were also modeling a message about inclusion and working with Blacks in the roles of authority. And some deranged bigot sought to mess up our performance by throwing pamphlets congratulating our oppressors."

I took a breath. Getting it off my chest helped. But talking things through and hearing their interpretations gave me a wider lens.

As they shared stories about how much heat they took from being an interracial couple in cosmopolitan London, I saw that the former Thirteen Colonies and Great Britain were still developing, growing up, so to speak, as civilizations, trying to come to terms with their empire-building brutality and enslavement of other human beings. But I also had to admit that as a nation, we were so segregated and divided that some people could not acknowledge the cruelty and hatred and the economic advantages of this system. Even pointing it out could become a problem in the United States of Amnesia. That's why human beings invented theater. And the NEC knew what they were doing. From a professional point of view, the work we performed was perfected to the point that nothing could disrupt or compromise the event. Everyone in the entire company delivered.

So many are still alive and active more than fifty years later. As for *The Song of the Lusitanian Bogey*, it continued to roar, disrupt, and upset people and make them think and feel in new ways. The play broke barriers and crossed a few borders. It proved influential in getting the South African miners a decent wage.

After I had been overseas with Janis and her tour, I wanted to bring my family abroad. I had done my homework. While I worked as a staff musician at ABC, I got to know Joe Wilder and Ernie Royal, who were in the same orchestra. They were experienced veterans who had toured Europe, so I asked them for advice. Joe, whose wife was from Sweden, helped me arrange travel for Mary and our daughters.

So, after the Negro Ensemble Company finished its tour in Rome, I bought a used 1958 Mercedes Benz and drove across the Alps and into Paris. What a car! After a few days hanging out and taking photographs, I headed for Luxembourg, where I had arranged to meet Mary and our three oldest girls: Lynn, age ten; Leslie, who just turned eight; and Mikey, who would soon celebrate her sixth birthday. We thought Stephanie was too young to travel with us, but we found that many families had brought their younger children along without serious problems. Live and learn. It's the fate of all parents.

We drove back to Paris and stayed for a week.

My old Chicago friend from childhood, Melvin Van Peebles, now a writer and filmmaker, had an apartment in central Paris. His girlfriend, Rosemary Wilbank, still lived there. We had previously arranged to leave the girls there overnight. Mary and I rented a room in a small hotel on the Left Bank, later used in the movie *Round Midnight*, which starred Dexter Gordon as an American musician living in Paris. The place was intimate and comfortable but not luxurious; it was right in the center of a lot of social activity. The AACM from Chicago was playing in Paris, and a few stayed in the same hotel. It was old home week.

Mary and I spent much time with drummer Steve McCall and his wife.

We got up each morning, walked across town to pick up the kids, enjoyed the city until late, and took them back at night to sleep. We got to see the hippest parts of the city. All the museums and famous sites were within easy walking distance or short Metro rides. We got better and better at enjoying ourselves. But that was just the beginning of our adventure.

We left Paris in that old Mercedes, headed straight south across the Pyrenees, and wound up on the outskirts of Barcelona. We checked into an old hotel and had an elegant room with tile floors and a separate room for the girls. Our stay for two nights was $30 in American money. When we sat for dinner, the owner-chef treated us to our first taste of Sangria as we celebrated Mikey's sixth birthday.

We attended a bullfight the next day. My daughter Lynn wound up rooting for the bull. A woman who understood English sought to pull her coat, but from our point of view, it was just plain cruelty to animals. Meanwhile, ever the architecture fan, my eyes wandered to a strange looking building on the horizon.

"La Sagrada Familia," a man with a son sitting next to me said, "designed by Antonio Gaudi. Construction had begun before I was born, and I hope my son will be alive to see its completion." Just a few years ago while on tour, I returned to the city and saw that the church had doubled in size and was still being worked on.

After we left Barcelona, we drove to Rome to take in all the sites and museums we could manage. The food was magnificent, and the atmosphere was warm and friendly. A week later, under a full moon, we crossed the Alps back into France. We arrived in Paris and camped out with Rosemary for a couple of days.

Everything had worked out as planned. I had enough money to get on the Metro to Place de L'Opera near the American Express office. I had given my brother $500 to wire me at American Express in Paris. The money was there, and we arrived home in style. I had the car shipped back to the U.S. We took a train to Luxembourg and then flew back to New York.

On the flight, I reflected on how our girls were now thoroughly American in their tastes. I recalled them complaining about the menu and craving a hot dog, hamburger, or pizza slice. That took me back to the complaints my brother Frank and I had about having to wear French berets and knickers. We never realized or appreciated that we were ahead of the curve. I'm glad I remember those times. It sure helps to understand your children better and grandchildren even more so.

As our parents had done with us, Mary and I exposed our kids to everything we were involved in and let them determine their personal preferences. Exposure didn't seem to harm any of them. I don't see any fear of inhibition in that generation at all.

What's both irreplaceable and indelible is the memory of a subtle smile on each child's face when they enjoyed some unexpected experience. The memories recur now when I see traces of my girls' actions in my grandchildren's behavior. This type of generational, oral/aural history reminds me that culture is a living, growing entity that is ever-changing. It will not stand still. It absorbs every influence as part of its overall synthesis.

Those first two visits to Europe—touring with Janis and touring with the NEC and my family—were positive in so many ways. I wound up going on a European tour every other year over the next few decades with a variety of musical performers, including Tony Williams, Gil Evans, Sam

Rivers, Aretha Franklin, M'Boom, Julius Hemphill, and Muhal Richard Abrams.

After a few seasons, I noticed a pattern of declining considerations, with both the income and the accommodations. Even with the big-name groups, jobs involving mostly (or most of) white American artists paid better. Those groups involving all Black American artists paid the least, as far as sidemen were concerned. I also noted that if a certain Black group came to the same overseas venue three times in close succession, the accommodations and financial compensation diminished each time. It seemed advisable to skip a venue a few years before returning. The more commercial white groups didn't seem to suffer such treatment.

When you're on the road with older and experienced musicians who pioneered this music, and you visit with younger and lesser experienced musicians enjoying better accommodations in the same hotel, it can mess with your head. Managing one's morale is always a good idea, but hospitality matters, especially in other countries. Musicians are sensitive people. To help them deliver their best, it's wise for one's hosts to take care of business and do things the right way.

Future engagements with a veteran like Max Roach taught me what these experiences should or could be with proper management. And Max had to do a lot of that himself. He was experienced enough to know what to request when traveling abroad. Touring with him in Europe was a real eye-opener.

He was the next musical pioneer who was about to change my life.

# CHAPTER 24

## *Max Roach & M'Boom*

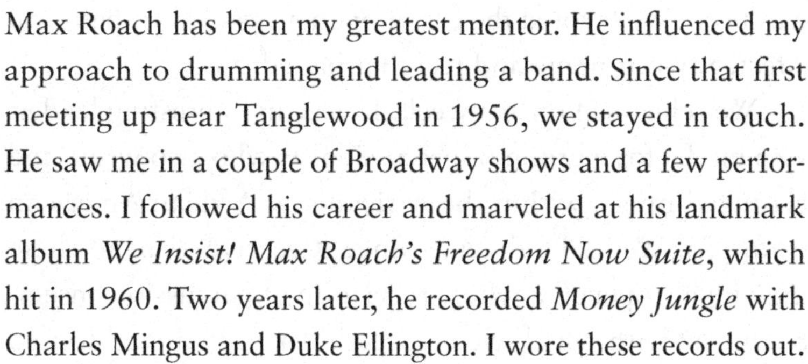

Max Roach has been my greatest mentor. He influenced my approach to drumming and leading a band. Since that first meeting up near Tanglewood in 1956, we stayed in touch. He saw me in a couple of Broadway shows and a few performances. I followed his career and marveled at his landmark album *We Insist! Max Roach's Freedom Now Suite*, which hit in 1960. Two years later, he recorded *Money Jungle* with Charles Mingus and Duke Ellington. I wore these records out.

During that same year of '62, my buddy Perk became Max's choral conductor and arranger for music that Max did with choirs and Abbey Lincoln on those Impulse records, like *It's Time*. Having been given special permission to attend this private recording session, I had a chance to talk with Max a little bit. He shared his vision of an African American percussion ensemble playing traditional African American music. He wanted each group member to be an excellent (and multiple) percussion instrumentalist as well as a composer and arranger.

A few years later, Max invited me to talk about people who might fit the bill musically and could deal with the ensemble professionally. In 1969 we rounded up four excellent musicians: Roy Brooks, Omar Clay, Joe Chambers, and Freddie Waits. We tried to recruit Jack DeJohnette, but he was on tour with Miles Davis.

Max knew that I had a drum kit, marimba, timpani, vibraphone, and a set of gongs at Studio WIS because his band rehearsed there all the time. I offered my studio space, agreed to coordinate the rehearsals, and find us some gigs.

M'Boom (pronounced "um boom" to sound like a drum) was born. We favored the use of onomatopoeia for rhetorical effect. Say our name and feel that bass drum.

We rehearsed once a week. It was an interesting leadership model for a group of percussionists who also wrote and arranged music within the African and African American tradition. We had a diverse range. Creative ideas of these individuals opened a whole repertoire of percussion ensemble music with which we recorded, performed, and toured internationally for the next twenty-nine years.

Max told us, "If we put everybody together and form a cooperative group, we'll have to stay together." He was right.

We not only stayed together, but we developed an original personality in percussion that came out of our combined musical experience. The origin for a tune might be the blues or gospel, but we approached it with an open-ended attitude.

Ultimately, we blended rather than were bound by traditions. But we were bound by ego. How could we define where the beat was when each drummer had a different beat? We were bandleaders. Three of us had master's degrees in percussion: Omar Clay, Fred King, and myself. King also had a doctorate in music. We were all used to being nothing but right all the damn time! Only someone of Max's mastery could define for us where the beat was.

In terms of working with Max, Freddie Waits said it best: "Max had been my childhood idol, and that call from him was the first time I had spoken to him on a person-to-person level. Not only did he ask me to be part of his organization, but he was also saying that it was supposed to be a cooperative organization. He did not want to be the principal figure, although we accept him as that because of who he is and what he has done. To watch a man of that humility who accepts all of us as equals on the bandstand is another incredible thing."

At first, Max was the only thing that kept us interested in each other. But his leadership was all about us building the music together. When one of us brought in a composition, Max made sure we submerged our egos (as great jazz stylists), listened with an open mind, and responded. We grew to be sensitive and excellent musicians in that personal sense.

A distinguishing feature of our ensemble was that we never brought any written music on stage. Max wanted nothing obstructing the audience's view, so we agreed to memorize everything. It may have given the impression to some viewers that we couldn't read music or that we were improvising everything and didn't know the techniques we used to play these instruments. However, that impression changed once we started playing. The music blended so well that it was clear we knew what we were doing.

The other reason M'Boom worked was the range of backgrounds and skills.

Freddie Waits, born in Jackson, Mississippi, was an accomplished flutist and a terrific composer, percussionist, and drummer. He had performed and recorded with "Ivory Joe" Hunter, Percy Mayfield, Stevie Wonder, Sonny Rollins, and Lena Horne.

Joe Chambers, born in Chester, Pennsylvania, was an excellent pianist, vibraphonist, arranger, and composer. He had recorded with Charles Mingus, Sonny Rollins, Donald Byrd, Archie Shepp, and under his own name.

Detroit-born Roy Brooks brought something that defies language. He played a musical saw. He played steel drums. He came at the music from such a novel dimension. He had performed and recorded with Horace Silver, Yusef Lateef, Charles Mingus, James Moody, Wes Montgomery, and Sonny Stitt. He also formed his own groups: Artistic Truth and the Aboriginal Percussion Choir.

St. Louis-born and Ohio-raised Omar Clay worked in orchestra pits for Broadway shows, opera, and symphonic work. He taught at New York's High School of Music and Arts. He had performed and recorded with Sarah Vaughan, Roberta Flack, Dionne Warwick, and many more.

We had all crossed a few borders. Being multifaceted and original composers, all this material worked. Moreover, though we were already established at our chosen percussion chair, we returned to the woodshed and grew additional percussion skills.

Before our first gig, we rehearsed for six months. During this time, we made some changes. Because we were not experts at African or conga drums, we brought in Richard Pablo Landrum. He gave us the sound we needed, but over time a personality conflict arose between him and Max. In short, he split.

We added conguero Ray Mantilla. What a great sound! He understood the subtle nuances in African, Latin, and jazz-based music. He had performed and recorded with Machito, Eddie Palmieri, Ray Barretto, Gato Barbieri, Charles Mingus, Art Blakey, Dizzy Gillespie, Marvin Gaye, and Herbie Mann. Ray adapted beautifully to our ensemble.

As Ray put it, "I had known Max Roach for years and worked with him on the Freedom Now Suite. So Joe Chambers came down and saw me with Art Blakey and told me they just happened to need my skill set. Being a percussionist from the Latin community who played with different jazz drummers, I felt like I had played with the top jazz drummers in the world.

Now I'm with the greatest of them. These are the cats. Max is, to me, the super drummer of the world."

The first time Ray played with us, it was seamless. Among other things, what impressed me was that he could solo on bongos, congas, or timbales and hold the audience. He was also funny as an emcee. When we performed in Spain, he introduced each one of us with quips and jokes in Spanish.

We needed another primary timpanist other than myself so I could be freed up to do other things; we also needed another mallet voice. That's when Fred King joined us as the eighth original member. Max knew him from his work in Puerto Rico. Fred had been teaching and playing in San Juan and had just returned to New York.

Trained in theory composition, conducting, and ethnomusicology with advanced degrees from the University of Iowa and the Julliard School, Fred had initiated a school of percussion while with Noah Greenberg's New York Pro Musica. He had organized percussion studies programs for the late Pablo Casals in Puerto Rico as Casals' first and only professor of percussion. He had performed with distinguished jazz and pop artists and as a solo timpanist and/or principal percussionist with many orchestras, including the New York City Opera and the Festival Casals Orchestra.

Fred spoke for all of us when he told the European press: "What excites me the most is that this band is a school. There's a spirit here. It doesn't matter where you come from or what you bring with you—you'll have to go to school. And there's an attitude that you will go to school. You will take criticism, but you always know that the criticism is given because you're seeking to grow. There's a camaraderie unlike any other musical group I've ever been in, whether it was a jazz group, symphony orchestra, or studio band. There has never been such a spirit of wanting to grow, and also blessed to have the masters around you to grow in that endeavor."

Putting M'Boom in historical context, Fred noted: "The percussion ensembles that have proliferated throughout the States are based on the European-American tradition. That is, they tend to lean more heavily on notated music. There may be some open-ended pieces where you can improvise, but I haven't seen anything approaching what we do in which we improvise with all the elements. That's not to imply that our music isn't highly structured or technical, but there is room for improvisation. And not only can we improvise with drums, but we're able to get that same effect with all the percussion instruments. I needed the freedom that M'Boom offered me to explore my creativity. With all due respect to the Zubin Mehtas of the classical world, their music doesn't offer me this kind of involvement."

Varese's Ionisation and Roldan's Ritmicas are considered the earliest percussion ensemble music in the European-American classical tradition. I played these compositions and others with Professor Price's ensemble at U of I. Yes, they are challenging pieces to sight read, and the idea is to deliver the same performance note for note. It's all about duplicating the score. Three hundred years from now, that music will sound essentially the same. By contrast, in the future, when people play M'Boom's music and follow our tradition—when they improvise—they will be defining the temper of the times.

What we were doing improvisationally was what we were feeling emotionally. That's why it can't be duplicated; it's a richer, more musician-engaged experience. As historians familiar with the traditional sounds of our profession, we were experimenting and changing, using bits of everything from all over the world.

"All the pieces are written in terms of textures, combinations of colors, and rhythmic structure or rhythmic feel—where we place the emphasis. We can play a tune in a couple of multi-meters, and it can be conceived as a three, a four, a six, or a twelve, depending on how we want it to feel at that time," Omar Clay said regarding composing for a percussion ensemble.

Joe Chambers expressed a similar feeling: "I just break percussion down into three or four categories: How do I get a bass line? How do I get chordal accompaniment? What do I use for melodic possibilities? You've got rhythm, so you break it down. Timpani and low marimba give you your bass line possibilities. The mallet instruments give you chordal and melodic possibilities, and, of course, you've got the drums. So that's one way to approach it. Another is about mood and texture. You could have all wood sounds, or all metal sounds, or all membranes, or different combinations."

Sitting in the audience, one saw eight players delivering a wide spectrum of sound: a set of five timpani, two concert grand marimbas, two drum sets, and a full complement of African drums, all courtesy of the Ludwig company. Add a vibraphone, xylophone, glockenspiel, gongs, bells, shakers, orchestra chimes, finger drums, steel drums, and a musical saw. That's what the stage looked like.

Our first performance was at Hempstead High School on Long Island in 1970. My percussion student, Napoleon Revels-Bey, taught music there. From 1969 through 1971, I taught Napoleon at nearby Adelphi University.

We did so well that first time out that I arranged for the second gig at Adelphi.

The second show really clinched it. Something incredible happened with that audience. It felt like an equal opportunity experience of awe. A listener didn't need to know anything about music to enter the state of mind we delivered.

After that, Max secured some European tours. It's no understatement to say that Max's name opened doors and rolled out red carpets. At one point, M'Boom played on Drum Day at the Newport Jazz Festival in the early Seventies. Groups led by Gene Krupa, Tony Williams, and Elvin Jones performed on the same bill. Papa Jo Jones presented a solo on high-hat that I still remember. Thanks to Max, we also appeared at the 1994 Monterey Jazz Festival.

Although the length of each tour varied, being on the road brought us even more together. The respect and admiration we felt for one another was solid. Yes, Max was our leader, but we all led, listened, and contributed in significant ways.

In the States, we often played on a double concert bill with either the Piano Choir (Sonelius Smith, Danny Mixon, Harold Mabern, Hugh Lawson, Ron Burton, Nat Jones, Stanley Cowell, Webster Lewis) or the World Saxophone Quartet (Julius Hemphill, Oliver Lake, Hamiet Bluiett, David

Murray). Among the highest compliments I remember from the press was that we were more melodic than the World Sax Quartet. Like us, the saxophonists and pianists found intriguing ways into ensemble playing.

These M'Boom concerts worked so well. Partly, it was that we defied expectation, delivered surprises, showcased virtuosity, and improvised with grace and fury. Partly, it was our preparation. We memorized everything, and we each brought an understudy on our tours who acted as a roadie but could fill in if we missed the gig. Partly, it was our stage full of instruments. The combination of the musical and the visual enhanced our impact. We had a kind of mystical effect on our audiences. We bridged African and world music with jazz compositions and improvisations. In short, we put a spell on you.

We recorded *Re:Percussion* for Baystate (1973), *M'Boom* for Columbia (1979), *Collage for Soul Note* (1984), *To the Max!* for Enjja (1991), and *Live at S.O.B.'s New York* for Blue Moon (1992). Besides the original eight, Eli Fountain, Craig McIver, Eddie Allen, Francisco Mora Catlett, Kenyatte Abdur-Rahman, Bobby Sanabria, and Steve Barrios have also graced the stage and recording studio as members of M'Boom.

We stayed active until 1998. Max passed away in 2004.

It was the gig of a lifetime and truly the crowning experience of my musical career. I've learned more about percussion (what to do and what not to do) as a member of M'Boom than in all the years I've been playing with other bands. I am sure that's true for every one of us. We loved performing this music. For me, it was the ultimate percussion ensemble experience in a career of many percussion ensembles stretching back to my undergrad days. I recorded and archived M'Boom's performances so future generations could know the magic.

As uplifting as our performances were and as wide as we found our audience to be, we did not tour as much as we would have liked. Because M'Boom was a side gig for all of us, we had to work around teaching and other touring schedules. Had we been together enough to find the right management, we could have relieved Max from the business side and let him concentrate on the artistic side. He should never have been saddled with accommodations, booking, and scheduling.

To put M'Boom's popularity in context, I remember in 1997 we did a concert in an opera coliseum in Italy. Tony Williams and Ginger Baker were featured soloists, along with Max Roach, accompanied by M'Boom. That may seem an unlikely combination, but Ginger was not out of place in such a setting.

We were scheduled to do a studio recording of the music in New York, but Tony Williams passed away (from a heart attack, after a routine gall bladder surgery) a day before the recording was to take place.

Tony was 51 years old. What might have happened.

# CHAPTER 25

## *Tony Williams, Ken McIntyre & SUNY/Old Westbury*

I am always surprised by fortuitous events. How one thing leads to another.

Playing the saxophone led to drum lessons from Oliver S. Coleman. That gave me a solid foundation as a sight reader and drummer. Playing in the family band led to my playing in the high school concert band and marching band, as well as Captain Dyett's summer concert band. Likewise, study with Professor Paul Price and working in his percussion ensemble, especially with John Cage, gave me an excellent foundation in avant-garde music and led me to Harry Partch's soundscapes.

Every one of these experiences led to my success in my master's degree program, which led to *West Side Story*, Johnny Richards, the ABC Orchestra, and Gil Evans. Drumming for Ken Makanda McIntyre led to Sam Rivers. Little did I know at the time the degree to which these avant-garde composers would prepare me for the most challenging and educational experiences in my career. Playing percussion in The Tony Williams Lifetime and the Max Roach-led percussion ensemble M'Boom turned out to be my performance equivalent of a Ph.D.

No question, Tony Williams was the other drummer besides Max who really changed my life. To my appreciation, Max helped invent bebop drumming, a major revolution in the music, and Tony Williams helped invent fusion drumming, the next evolution in the music.

I first heard Tony in 1961. I was in Boston on a two-week engagement as Nat King Cole's percussionist. A group of us, including our drummer Leon Pettis, drove over after the show, hoping to catch Herb Pomeroy's big band with my friend, the great Alan Dawson, playing drums. I knew I would learn something new from hearing Alan with such an ensemble.

Of course, we were disappointed to find out that Alan wasn't there, especially when he learned his replacement was a fourteen-year-old student of his. We weren't disappointed long.

I learned something that night, all right. I'm sure glad that another drummer witnessed it with me.

This kid scared the shit out of me.

I immediately realized that this teenager had raised the standard by which all drummers would be evaluated. I knew I had to reinvent myself if I wanted to continue playing the drums.

He sent my ass back to the woodshed. It took me three years of daily practice in my studio to regain my confidence and self-assurance as a drummer. My percussion chops were okay, and I continued to build my reputation in that respect. But my first love has always been the drums, and I had to raise my level to keep getting calls for that instrument.

Tony was thirteen when he did his first professional gigs with Sam Rivers. I caught Tony a few years later when he played with Jackie McLean. Tony's innate talent, something that comes along maybe once or twice in a generation, was still growing.

At seventeen, he joined that mid-Sixties Miles Davis band (Second Great Quintet). To my appreciation, that band was centered around Tony. His inventive technique as a drummer was so out front. The metric modulations, the crisp delivery, the polyrhythmic riot, and that rapid but light swing. Although everyone in that band—Miles, Herbie Hancock, Wayne Shorter, Ron Carter—were great improvisers, Tony fed them little tastes that took their solos further.

The one thing those albums did not show was Tony's considerable talent as a composer. After he left Miles, much more of his recorded music was his material. The arrangements, as well. His first version of The Tony Williams Lifetime was a trio with British guitarist John McLaughlin and the magical Larry Young, Jr, a second-generation organist. *Emergency!*, a double album released in 1969, is considered by many to be the pioneering classic of jazz fusion. A year later, Jack Bruce joined the band for *Turn It Over*. Tony would make many personnel changes over the years.

In 1971, Tony called me on the recommendation of my old friend and musical associate Howard Johnson. He was assembling a new version of Lifetime and needed a third percussionist. He was on the drum kit; Don Alias was on congas and African percussion. I was to play vibes, marimba, timpani, gongs, bells, and bass drum. I was all in.

Tony scheduled two days, each with a three-hour rehearsal and a recording of the rehearsed material that evening. This is not an unusual schedule for studio recording or production (at least it wasn't then). Most recordings were done without any prior rehearsal. You are expected to show up on time, read through the music once while the engineer does the sound check, and record it.

All nine tracks on the album were Tony's compositions. We improvised a couple of percussion pieces in the final recording (and got credit). His tunes were well-developed, leaving a lot of room for exploration. And this was a band of explorers. The holdover from the first Lifetime, Larry Young, had citizenship on other planets. No star was too far from his reach. One eerie chord on his Hammond B3 organ and we were all in outer space. A more rock-oriented Ted Dunbar replaced John McLaughlin on guitar. Ron Carter replaced Jack Bruce on bass. Ron also played cello. The six of us completed the whole album in those two evenings.

Shortly after that, we (minus Ron) started doing some gigs around the city for a few months and then embarked on a European tour (plus Arthur Juini Booth on bass) that included the Montreux Jazz Festival in Switzerland. *Ego*, the name of the record, turned out great, but when we hit the road, playing almost every night, the music developed beyond belief.

Without a word, Tony started playing. We only knew what song he played by what he did on the drum set. We all found our way into the music, and things started to cook. But in the middle of any song, he might break into a different tune. Like a deer that leaped and changed direction in mid-air, Tony never broke his stride. The whole ensemble ran with him seamlessly. Throughout this shifting sonic adventure, our intuition antennae grew. We were most definitely crossing musical borders and pioneering new sounds.

Every performance was different and far more imaginative than the record. It was tight but with no obvious sign of conducting or leading, just one huge graceful, beautiful sound parade. I often had the chance to sit behind or beside Tony and absorb what he did and how. It changed my playing forever. He just willed his way right through the most impossible shit imaginable. Too fast? Too complicated? I'll make you hear it. And he always did.

There were times when he played some strange and seemingly abstract passage. I thought to myself, "Now what the hell was that? Why'd he play that?" The form evolved, and at that spot he played the strange passage again. Then I'd realize that I just hadn't understood it the first time I heard it. That's how he worked. The Tony Williams Lifetime was an apt title for his ensembles and his inimitable concept of music. It's taken me a lifetime to catch up to this cat.

He went on to form many more versions of Lifetime right up until his untimely death in 1997.

Playing with Tony Williams coincided with another major change in my life. In 1971 Ken Makanda McIntyre created the (first of its kind) African American music and performing arts program at the State University of New York (SUNY) on the Old Westbury campus on Long Island.

I had been teaching music as an associate professor and chairing the Black Studies Department at nearby Adelphi University for the last two years, but Ken's offer to join his faculty was a once-in-a-lifetime opportunity. Ken also brought in his protégé, Richard Harper, a Detroit native who had studied with Ken at Wesleyan University. In fact, the former president at Wesleyan, now the president of SUNY/ Old Westbury, supported Ken's developing of the performing arts program. Ken, Richard, and I ran it. We added dance teachers: first Betty Barney, then Denise Braithwaite.

Ken earned his Doctorate of Music in curriculum design from the University of Massachusetts at Amherst in 1975. It was a program Max Roach had begun. Ken stayed at Old Westbury until he retired in 1995. Richard and I retired a year later when the college administration retrenched the whole program.

We strongly believe that the decision was political. After all, our work was tremendously popular on campus. We provided live music for every dance concert and theater performance that required it. Although we were never adequately funded, we performed beyond expectations each year. Our faculty consisted of people with considerable professional experience. We graduated musicians who went on to careers as composers, arrangers, performers, and educators.

Despite our program's success, the SUNY system wanted to establish its flagship performing arts at the new campus in Purchase, New York, an hour or so north of the city. Our program provided a four-year performance degree focused on African American music, dance, and theater, the only such concentration in the entire 67 colleges of the SUNY system. As for SUNY/Old Westbury, it never put another performing arts program into its curriculum. In fact, the new university president told me after my retirement that the system would give him money to do anything else except that.

But by the 1990s, jazz programs had caught on at the university level. When Ken left Old Westbury, he and Reggie Workman began teaching in the program set up by Chico Hamilton in The New School for Social Research in downtown Manhattan. Richard Harper joined them on the faculty the next year.

# CHAPTER 26

## *The AACM, Bells & BAG*

The early Seventies was a coming together of creative forces, seen and unseen.

I taught music, recorded music, played in bands, and led my own band. In 1973, Strata-East produced *Warren Smith and the Composer's Workshop Ensemble*, our first LP. The following year they produced *We've Been Around*. In 1978, Baystate produced *Folks Songs*, our third LP.

Studio WIS shifted gears. Into the Seventies, the experimentation grew wider. In part, it was due to new arrivals like avant-garde trumpeter-composer Leo Wadada Smith, who studied at Wesleyan, and saxophonist-composer Oliver

Lake who studied at Yale. They needed a performance space free of hassles. We were glad to provide it.

Just as I had come to New York in the late 1950s with a group of Chicago musicians like percussionist Michael Colgrass and bassist Dave Moore, Black Arts Group (BAG) musicians and composers had followed Oliver Lake out of St. Louis in the early Seventies. They arrived en masse: Julius Hemphill, Hamiet Bluiett, JD Parran, James Jabbo Ware, among others. These cats could play!

I started working with all of them. In 1973, I became the drummer in saxophonist-composer Jabbo Ware's large ensemble, The Me We and Them Orchestra, yet another band I stayed with for decades. Saxophonist-composer Julius Hemphill hit New York in the mid- Seventies. We began to play duets in concert. He played the hell out of that saxophone. We recorded a couple of albums for Black Saint Records and toured Europe.

Leo Wadada Smith, like my doo-wop singing homie Kalaparush Difda (then Maurice McIntyre), had been a member of the Association for the Advancement of Creative Musicians (AACM). My brother, Frank, was a member, too, along with other visual artists.

When I visited Chicago, Frank invited me to a concert by the AACM orchestra. The first piece was a composition by Wadada called "Bells." The orchestra waited for everything to be quiet. Conductor Muhal Richard Abrams took a tiny bell and started ringing it; another musician rang a bell, then another until all the musicians were ringing bells of different sizes and sounds. It grew into an uproar and rose to a supercharged volume level. Horns were added one by one, and then it went back down again until there was only one bell. Then absolute silence.

What an ecstatic state they produced! Because of the way the sound evolved, we were all transported. It was as if our ears had been cleansed of clutter. Every sound was new. This was the kind of atmosphere I had been trying to create as well: a whole orchestra playing improvised music or structures created for improvisation. And every performance was different. I know because I borrowed "Bells" for use with my ensemble.

Having started the AACM in 1965 with Steve McCall, Phil Cohran, and Jodie Christian, Muhal arrived at Studio WIS in 1976. He composed for symphony orchestras, big bands, string quartets, piano, and large ensembles. He really connected with what I could do on timpani, marimba, vibraphone, and glockenspiel. I worked on four of his Black Saint albums throughout the Eighties. He often brought his former student, Henry Threadgill, to play and hang out.

Anthony Braxton was the next member of the AACM to make the scene. I remember my first recording date with him in 1976 for Creative Orchestra Music. Twenty-three musicians were gathered. I had come from another recording and was a few minutes late. The drummers were stumped by Anthony's symphonic orchestration, so when they saw Mr. Sight Reader arrive, they asked me to look it over. The chart wasn't really that hard. It turned out to be a great session. Still, this was early in the game. Many people were not yet aware of the range of Anthony's abilities as a composer, but they would soon find out.

Once again, the music crossed borders. Pioneers like Muhal and Anthony, Wadada and Oliver, the AACM and BAG, drew audiences from African American classical music and European American classical music. Studio WIS was in a right place/right time/right fit with these innovators of free jazz. Through the Seventies into the Nineties, we also drew many percussion and drum students (and teachers) throughout the metropolitan area.

From 1970-'76, I played on a lot of recordings, many deeply gratifying. Because of the work I had done in the Sixties with percussion instrumentation in various musical settings, more composers and arrangers knew what I could provide in the studio.

Among the most memorable sessions were dates with Sonny Terry and Brownie McGee, Sam Rivers' Tuba Trio, a duet with Japanese saxophonist Hidefumi Toki, Roberta Flack, Judy Collins (Whales and Nightingales), Donny Hathaway, Art Farmer, Rahsaan Roland Kirk, Gene Ammons, Sonny Stitt, Kenny Barron, Hubert Laws, Herbie Mann, Dick Griffin, Billy Harper, Enrico Brava, David Sanborn, Gary Burton and Mike Gibbs, Talib Hakim, Charles Tolliver, Jimmy Owens, Joe Zawinul, The Last Poets, Blood, Sweat and Tears, and the original Broadway cast recording of Ntozake Shange's brilliant musical choreo-poem "For Colored Girls Who Have Considered Suicide When the Rainbow Is Enuf."

Playing with Count Basie's band on *Afrique* was one of my biggest thrills. Producers, having never encountered a timpanist with a jazz background, made excellent use of the instrument on this Africa-inspired LP. I couldn't believe my good luck. Playing on a record with the Basie band was a childhood dream come true. It was another shot of serendipity.

After the record date, guest arranger Oliver Nelson (check his "Stolen Moments") hired me to play percussion in his big band. Nelson was writing a symphonic work in residency at his alma mater, Washington University in St. Louis. Deeply involved in jazz education, he impressed me as a composer-arranger-saxophonist beyond borders. I was not surprised to learn of his multiple success in writing and arranging Hollywood film scores.

My timpani playing also came to the attention of drummer Elvin Jones, another of my idols. I played on his *The Prime Element* along with Candido Camero (congas), Omar Clay, and Richard Pablo Landrum (percussion) and a great lineup of sax players.

Although I thoroughly enjoyed the Anything Goes experimentation of those mid-to-late Sixties recording sessions, these sessions in the Seventies took fuller advantage of the range of my percussion work.

# CHAPTER 27

## *Lena Horne, Quincy Jones & Senegal*

I've never had to beg for a gig, but I did have to speak up once.

My old buddy Perk was the writer-arranger of a Broadway musical, and I was his first choice in the percussion chair. The contractor called me several times at Studio WIS—not to confirm me but to replace me with another percussionist. Technology alert: cell phones and the internet had not yet come into use. My studio, a common meeting place for artists, often received such calls.

Finally, during one such call, I asked him, "When are you going to call me?"

He stuttered, hung up, and left my question unanswered. But with persistence, I got the job, the Broadway show *Lena Horne, the Lady and Her Music*. It hit in May of 1981 and ran for twenty months. Then it toured nationally. Then it toured Canada and Sweden.

Unlike many bio-plays that turn a cultural pioneer into a cliché and their story into a yawn-fest, Lena's show brought out her ferocious warrior spirit. She entranced her audience. Her ninety-minute performance was her life journey from chorus girl under the wing of Noble Sissle to international icon and celebrity. The show was full of great tunes she had made famous. Her producer, Quincy Jones, understood that these songs became more meaningful to her audience in the context of the struggles and triumphs in her personal and professional life.

The set resembled a nightclub rather than a theatrical Broadway show, and Lena was right at home. She walked out on stage, stood at the microphone, radiated magnetism, and just belted it out. Consistent, efficient, professional, transcendent—nothing disturbed or distracted her. My daughters were in awe of her. So was I. Every night she sang with such incredible beauty and passion. The show was a victory lap of an extraordinary career; it reanimated and reinvigorated her.

Like Duke Ellington and Gil Evans, Quincy Jones has a feel for bringing out the best in his players, whether he's composing, arranging, conducting—or, in this case, producing. He certainly paved a most creative way for Ms. Horne. Every performance she gave was a celebration and a repudiation of all the forces that have tried to limit or deny her talent.

I've always admired the way Quincy works. I got to know him in the early Seventies while playing percussion on two of his fusion-soul-funk LPs: *Gula Matari* and *I Heard That!!* A year older than me, we were neighbors, a block away from one another in Chicago, but we didn't meet until years later in the Big Apple.

Q came up playing trumpet in Lionel Hampton's band, but he soon discovered he had an ear for arrangements. He studied composition and theory with Nadia Boulanger and Olivier Messiaen in Paris and became a music director for a record company there. Synthesizing all these musical influences, he began to write film scores. He conducted and arranged for singers like Frank Sinatra, Sarah Vaughan, and Ella Fitzgerald. He expanded the jazz tradition.

As a percussionist who relishes interpreting jazz idioms, I felt especially suited for playing in Quincy's ensembles.

The only problem with the Lena show was turf. Broadway shows are controlled by wealthy investors who get insecure easily. To be blunt: Perk got fired. However, his arrangements were used both on Broadway and on the album we recorded. It won the Grammy Award for Best Musical Theater Album. Quincy, producer of the musical and the album, accepted the award with Lena Horne, who also won the Grammy for Best Pop Vocal Performance Female. It was most deserved. They were both forces of nature. They created something truly powerful and awe-inspiring by working together.

As the Seventies gave way to the Eighties, my schedule in the recording studio grew less hectic. I not only liked the slower pace, I liked the jobs: Sam Rivers' groups, Jaki Byard,

Julius Hemphill's quartet, Bill Cole's ensemble, Noel Pointer's Disco Concierto, David Sanborn, Marion Brown, Anthony Davis, the Muhal Richard Abrams Orchestra, the Vincent Chancey Trio (with bassist Wilber Morris and Vincent on French horn), the Grover Mitchell Orchestra, and M'Boom. My band, Composer's Workshop Ensemble, recorded *Cricket Song-Poem* for Miff Music in 1982.

In the fall of 1981, Mary passed away.

Man, it hit me hard. Nothing had ever stopped me before. I was shaken.

Once the intense grieving passed and I could actually compose a letter, I wrote my four daughters Lynn, Leslie, Mikey, and Stephanie. I shared that when I fell in love with their mother, I was in completely—hook, line, sinker, and rod—until death did us part. I pointed out that I knew her as no other person knew her, and she knew me like no one else because we talked everything over during our thirty-three years together.

I met her when I was fourteen (she was only eleven), and by my twenty-first year, I realized she had me for as long as she wanted me. We spent two years in college courting, then seven more developing into a family unit, and the next seventeen years watching the roots and branches of our family tree spread and flower all around us. I told our children to commemorate Mary. She was goodness incarnate, and everyone who knew her felt it. I added that we will circulate her love of life, strength, and energy to those who need it. I reminded them that there is no cause for sorrow. Mary has moved on to a higher place, away from the weight of the troubles we knew together, yet the essence of her life lives on in us.

Despite my encouraging note to my daughters, I still grieved Mary's loss for a long time. What pulled me through was my two lifelong allies: my family and playing the music.

A few years later, I married my second wife, Patricia Lucille Hall, a dancer, choreographer, teacher, and the mother of Nairobi, our daughter.

Even though we both were New Yorkers, we settled in Newark. I moved from Hempstead, Long Island. For me, Newark spelled relief. Traveling on Long Island highways to class and to gigs in my Mercedes Benz (the drum kit fit snugly), I had to add extra time because I was stopped so frequently by local law enforcement. Perhaps the police confused me with trouble. Why were they suspicious of a Black man driving an expensive foreign car?

Newark is a different story. It's not a town dominated by commuters but a city in its own right. It has culture, history, and heritage. Though it's relatively easy and quick to get to Manhattan, I discovered that some of my neighbors never even crossed the Hudson River.

In the summer of 1987, Pat and I (and Nairobi) toured Europe. Pat taught dance, I taught music, and we performed together as well. Everything went superbly, and we had the chance to visit Dakar, Senegal, for a short side trip, made possible by my old friend and fellow percussionist Anton

Reid and his wife Ariane Reid, who had been living there for a few years.

Like many African Americans making their first trip to Mother Africa, many things seemed eerily familiar: the faces in the markets, the sounds of children playing in the street. It was like being transported to my grandparents' home and neighborhood in Maywood, Illinois, in the 1940s.

These sense impressions of Senegal soon became "African Sketches," a composition recorded on Studio WIS: 20th Anniversary Concert in 1988, produced by Miff Music.

These impressions are still with me today.

# CHAPTER 28

## *Duke's Orchestra, Check's in the Mail & Sugar Hill*

Recalling the 1990s, playing with the Duke Ellington Orchestra comes to mind first. My old friend, Jack Jeffers, was now the orchestra's musical director. He was most influential in securing my tenure on the drum kit. Duke's son Mercer (and later Duke's grandson Paul Mercer Ellington) conducted.

That weekly gig at Birdland lasted for seven glorious years. What a book! What a band!

We played the early songs, the dance tunes, the symphonic works, Suite Thursday, the Far East Suite, the sacred music

Duke composed near the end of his life, and everything Billy Strayhorn and Mercer wrote.

Playing these compositions felt like I was coming home to the old South Side neighborhood. It was a "Moonglow" experience all over again. Drumming to these great charts with these first-call musicians was another career highlight for me. I could not have found a better way to immerse myself in the music of America's most prolific composer than with this orchestra.

As for recordings in the studio made in this decade, three stand out: *Peru Dream Sequence*, a project I composed, produced, and played vibes and percussion on, with Herb Bushler on bass, Eli Fountain on drums, and my buddy Perk on piano. On the second project, I was among forty musicians on *Cage/Cunningham*, an LP of electronic and experimental music composed by John Cage and Merce Cunningham (with my U of I Professor Paul Price, U of I grad Michael Colgrass, and me in the percussion ensemble).

The third project, *Cats Are Stealing My Shit* on Mapleshade Records, featured my compositions played by Steve Novosel on bass, Kent Jordan on flute, Chief Bey on percussion, Stanley Cowell on piano, and Amirou Willingham rapping. It was produced by Hamiet Bluiett. For some reason, this particular recording got a lot more attention, review-wise. Unlike the reach (and budget and leverage power) of the big record conglomerations, indie music companies have a tough time getting press, print or electronic. Genres like free jazz and avant-garde, whose beauty is in the ear of the beholder, benefit so much from critics who can get inside the music and give a magazine's readership an experience, or at least a taste, of the recording.

In the 1990s, I played percussion on *Untempered Trio* with Bill Cole on reeds, Joe Daley on baritone sax, tuba, and synthesizer; dueted with Julius Hemphill on saxes and flute on Chile New York; sat in with the David Ware Trio on *Passage to Music*. I played vibes and timpani on Muhal Richards' *Blu Blu Blu*; vibes, timpani, marimba and gong on Muhal's *Familytalk*; vibes, drums, percussion, and gong on saxophonist Andrew Lamb's *Portrait in the Mist*; timpani on Elvin Jones' *This Point in Time*; vibes on pianist Kenny Barron's *Soft Spoken Here: Sunset to Dawn/Golden Lotus*; drums on Jabbo Ware's *Today's Move* and *Heritage Is* and Ken McIntyre: *The Complete United Artists Sessions*; percussion on trumpeter Art Farmer's jazz funk *Gentle Eyes*, vocalist Nnenna Freelon's *Listen* and Anthony Braxton's *4 Ensemble Compositions*, and drums and percussion on *J.D. Parren & Spirit Stage*, among others.

The funniest episode of that era happened while we were recording New Orleans trumpeter-composer Terence Blanchard's score for *X*, Spike Lee's film version of *The Autobiography of Malcolm X*. I, one among seventy-six musicians, alternated playing drums and percussion. In the middle of a take, Spike came into the huge studio to say or do something and got tangled in a cable connected to Howard Johnson's tuba mic. As many of us watched with widening eyes, Howard and his tuba slowly tilted and then went over backward.

No doubt embarrassed, Spike panicked and said that "someone who had gotten high" had caused the accident. No one was hurt, but Spike had to be settled down. I guess he thought his reputation might be tarnished. Although his dad, Bill, was a famous jazz bassist, Spike grew highly concerned that jazz players on his record might be puffing. The entire orchestra couldn't stop laughing, so they had to give everyone a break.

In 1996, checks arrived in the mail with my name on them. These monthly retirement pension checks (from my twenty-five years teaching at SUNY/Old Westbury) suggested a life change. But rather than retire and sit on a beach, I realized the pension allowed me to pursue a wider range of musical options. Now that basics were covered, making records, composing music, rehearsing my band, and touring became a lot more fun.

I began to do percussion workshops. I combined a presentation, a performance, and a specific drum or percussion technique. I enjoyed giving workshops and playing with different ensembles. It was different than teaching in the same school every semester. I appreciated the intense focus.

The other benefit of the pension was the chance to bring my family closer. My children were all grown up, and sharing with my grandchildren the lessons I learned from Moms and Pops and Ma and Dad has become a favorite pastime.

As for Studio WIS, my experiments with avant-garde musical pioneers continued through the Nineties with multi-instrumentalist Bill Cole and his Untempered Ensemble, pianist-composer Cooper Moore, saxophonist-composer Andrew Lamb, and bandleader-saxophonist-composer David Ware.

In 1996, avant-garde bassist-composer William Parker and his wife Patricia Nicholson, a dancer and choreographer, began the Vision Festival on the Lower East Side. Featuring thirty to sixty acts, the four-day festival runs annually, every May to June. The timing of its inception was promising as the loft era came to an end. The duration of its run demonstrates how much the avant-garde benefits from cultural events that mix experimental music, art, film, and dance in their program.

In 1998 we moved into a Harlem apartment in a building that dates back to the days of the Harlem Renaissance in the neighborhood once called "Sugar Hill." It proved to be a great location for Pat and me because we both had plenty of work. When we first started, Pat was earning her master's degree. Now her career as a choreographer and dance teacher was taking off. Nairobi was in college, and I was playing, rehearsing, recording, teaching, and touring. It wasn't just "two careers and one car" that was the problem. We both were so busy that we each needed a partner with a less hectic lifestyle. We talked it over and came to the same conclusion. We ended our marriage but vowed always to be family. Pat met Pamela Patrick, her new life partner, and I met Debby Randolph, who would become my third wife. All are part of our extended family. Everyone gets along at Smith family gatherings and reunions. That includes Frank, his three daughters, and his three wives.

# CHAPTER 29

## *New Venues, New Century & Re-releases*

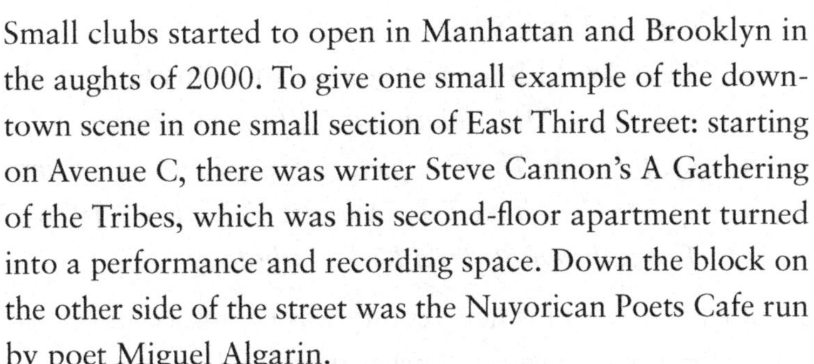

Small clubs started to open in Manhattan and Brooklyn in the aughts of 2000. To give one small example of the downtown scene in one small section of East Third Street: starting on Avenue C, there was writer Steve Cannon's A Gathering of the Tribes, which was his second-floor apartment turned into a performance and recording space. Down the block on the other side of the street was the Nuyorican Poets Cafe run by poet Miguel Algarin.

Further west and a tad south stood The Stone, run by avant-garde composer John Zorn, and then came the Bowery Poetry Club, run by poet Bob Holman. Each space offered dance, theatre, music, and poetry, often in collaboration. Another example of our musical tradition adjusting to the times was the opening in 2005 of the Middle School Jazz Academy under the auspices of Jazz at Lincoln Center. I joined the faculty and gave percussion and drum presentations. I especially appreciate that they offer tuition-free jazz instruction to middle school students from all over New York City. It's an uplifting program that gives young people at a formative age an authentic experience of what life in music is like.

As goes the new century, many recordings I had made in the previous century were remastered and re-released, often in new collections, box sets, or compilations:

- *Miles Davis and Gil Evans: The Complete Studio Recordings* (with seventeen tracks on which I played marimba and timpani) on Columbia
- *Muhal Richard Abrams: The Complete Remastered Recordings on Black Saint*
- *Julius Hemphill: The Complete Remastered Recordings on Black Saint*
- New World Records' box set of Julius Hemphill's *The Boye: Multi-National Call for Harmony*
- *J.J. Johnson: The Complete '60s Big Band Recordings*
- *Spirits Up Above: The Atlantic Years 1965-1976*
- *The Rahsaan Roland Kirk Anthology*

Another feature of the new century was the release of concert CDs, often of shows from earlier decades. For example:

- *Voodoo Chile* is a performance of the Gil Evans Orchestra live in Sweden in 1974 and in Germany in '78, tours I played on. In addition, many avant-garde recordings were getting produced in France, Germany, Italy, and Japan. The music was often made in New York clubs and recording studios but put together and released abroad.

» Regarding my own music, Freedom Art produced *Race Cards* in 2003. I composed and arranged seven of the songs; French horn player Mark Taylor wrote and arranged two more.

2005

» Engine Studios released *The Dogon Duo*, a duet with saxophonist Andrew Lamb, followed by *Natural/Cultural Forces* in 2007, a duet with Tom Abbs on bass, with guest appearances from Lamb and Taylor

2009

» Engine Studios put out *Old News, Borrowed Blues*, ten of my compositions played by my band Composer's Workshop Ensemble

2011

» Porter Records released my free-soul-funk jazz/spoken word/comic children's story with adult twists called *Dragon Dave Meets Prince Black Knight from the Dark Side of the Moon*
» Engine Studios released *Odd Time*, an experimental project with banjo player Eugene Chadbourne and me on timpani, vibes, marimba, and percussion

2014

» Joseph Daley's *Wispercussion/Five Portraits of Warren Smith*, I played jazz and classical solos

2016

- » I played the Vilnius Jazz Festival in Lithuania with fellow percussionist Arkadijus Gotesmanas and saxophonist Andrew Lamb

2017

- » No Business Records released our performance as *Sea of Modicum*.

As for work with other artists:

- » I was concertmaster for Salim Washington's Strings
- » I played drums on *Extremes and Musical Blessing* with the Kalaparush McIntyre Quartet
- » Kidd Jordan's *On Fire* and *On Fire 2*
- » *Nine Ways and Three Fifths*, composed and performed by bassist Paul Steinbeck (with Andrew Lamb on tenor sax, Niko Higgins on alto sax)
- » Rob Brown Trio (with Rob on alto saxophone and William Parker on bass) on *Round the Bend*
- » *Pomegranate* and *Live at the Festival of New Trumpet Music* with the Stephen Haynes Trio
- » Three of David Ware's projects (*Shakti*, *Onecept*, and *Theatre Garonne*)
- » *The Guiseppi Logan Quintet*, and on six LPs—three recorded live; three in the studio—with saxophonist-composer-arranger James Finn
- » I played vibes, marimba, gong, drums, and timpani on trumpeter Bill Dixon's *Envoi, Seventeen Musicians in Search of a Sound: Darfur, and Tapestries for Small Orchestra*

» Drums, percussion, and timpani on alto saxophonist Odeon Pope's *Universal Sounds*

» Drums, marimba and percussion on trumpeter Stephen Haynes' *Parrhesia*

» Balafon (a gourd xylophone from West Africa), bass marimba, vibes, temple block and drums on David Taylor's *Red Sea*

» Drums and percussion on *Tribute to Albert Ayler* (with saxophonist Joe McPhee, trumpeter Roy Campbell and bassist William Parker)

» I played percussion on trombonist J.J. Johnson's *Goodies*

» *Six Standards* by Anthony Braxton and Dave Douglas

» Percussionist on Reggie Nicholson's *Timbre Suite*

» I played percussion and trap drums on Bill Cole's *Seasoning the Greens*

» Drums, vibes, and percussion on Paul Steinbeck's *Sun Set*

» Vibes, marimba, and percussion in Joseph Daley's Earth Tones Ensemble in *The Seven Deadly Sins*

» Vibes and percussion on baritone saxophonist Claire Daly's *Heaven Help Us All*

» *Double Diploid* with the Steve Swell-David Taylor Quartet

» Vibes with the JC Hopkins Biggish Band on *Underneath a Brooklyn Moon*

» With multi-reedist, Marty Erlich's Large Ensemble on *A Trumpet in the Morning*

2019

» Aum Fidelity released a session I did with the David S. Ware New Quartet.

2020

» No Business Records released *The Spell*, a Vincent Chancey Trio live concert.

Looking back on recording dates from the 1950s to now, every session made me a better accompanist, no matter what I played or with whom I played. I started by working in a wide range of genres, but in each subsequent decade, the jobs got more focused on my particular talents. One of the unexpected benefits of playing with musicians over sixty years is that unique magic that comes with longevity. Like much of the work I did in the Nineties, the recordings in the new century are with musicians I have played with for a long time.

In short, whether in the studio or the bandstand, it only gets better.

# CHAPTER 30

## *Three More Generations Crossing Borders*

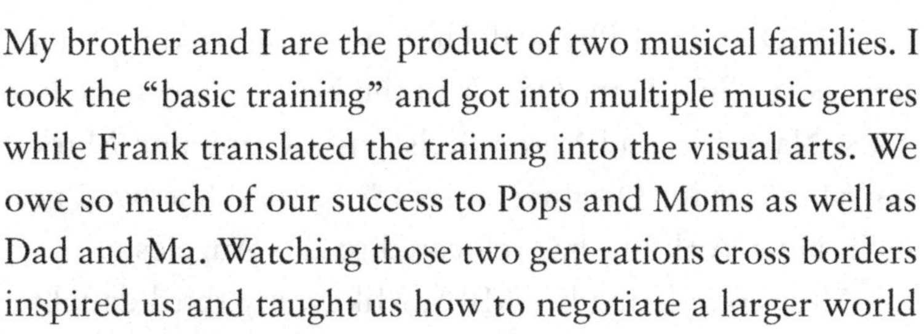

My brother and I are the product of two musical families. I took the "basic training" and got into multiple music genres while Frank translated the training into the visual arts. We owe so much of our success to Pops and Moms as well as Dad and Ma. Watching those two generations cross borders inspired us and taught us how to negotiate a larger world and our artistic place in it.

Likewise, I am inspired by my daughters and proud to be their father. All five have undergraduate degrees. Most have graduate degrees as well. Yes, they are the children of parents who are teachers, but our kids learned how to acquire knowledge because each succeeding child was taught by their older sisters. By the time they reached first grade, they knew how to thrive in school. I never had to pay for their college tuition. For the most part, they all earned scholarships to offset the cost.

My eldest daughter, Lynn, is a pediatrician and an Associate Professor of Pediatrics at her university. She has followed in my footsteps by making a career of teaching her craft. She is married to Herbert Smitherman, a physician who is also an academic, and they have two children. Their elder child, Kristen, is married to Emilio Voltaire; they have two children, Arya and Gianna. Sean, their son, has a daughter, Leyla.

Leslie, my second daughter, works as a senior executive coordinator at The Federal Home Loan Mortgage Corporation (Freddie Mac). Leslie is married to Feliciano (Tito) Mejia, a Patent Examiner with the U.S. Patent and Trademark Office. They have two daughters, Kaelin and Kelsey. Kaelin (Doctor of Physical Therapy) is married to Navon Jeffries, a Chief Petty Officer in the Navy. They have two sons, Navon Jr. and Kyren. Kelsey is a Campaign Marketing Manager for Original Series for Netflix. She lived near us in New York but has relocated to Los Angeles.

After completing her MBA, Mikey, my third daughter, helped develop eCommerce on the Internet for Intel. After seven years, she left Intel to form her own company. She is now the Chief Operating Officer for a law firm in Washington, DC. She met her husband, Will Koon, in the Army. He is a civilian attorney for the Army JAG Corps and a retired

Army Colonel. They have two children, Jordan, a performer in New York City, and Gabrielle who recently graduated from Shenandoah University summa cum laude.

Stephanie, my fourth daughter, teaches computer science and a STEAM/Makerspace program in middle school. She is married to Albert D. Walden, Jr. (Sandy). Coincidentally, as a child, I used to hear the story about John Walden and his dog Bandy who lived across the way from our homestead in North Carolina. It turns out that John Walden was Sandy's great-grandfather. Sandy and Stephanie have two children: Jade works for NJ Motor Vehicle Commission and Albert III (Tre) is a supervisor for Legend Biotech: a global, commercial-stage biotechnology company developing and manufacturing novel therapies. Tre has two daughters (Mya & Malia) with his wife, Rousel.

Nairobi, my fifth daughter, was recruited by IBM out of college and worked in Europe with them before returning to the U.S. She also operates her own company. Nairobi is married to Frank Kim, who is a renowned cyber security professional. Their two daughters, Nia and Nylah, are competitive gymnasts in the Junior Olympic program. They also welcomed a son into the world, Phoenix, just before the COVID-19 pandemic hit.

We now have eleven grandchildren and seven great-grandchildren. Five of our grandchildren have completed at least one university degree, and three are still finishing theirs. Because their mothers and I placed a high value on education, our grandchildren have benefited and passed this on to their children. Two of the three youngest have already traveled abroad with their parents and are bilingual, as their paternal grandparents are Korean.

Thanks to my elders, I also saw that even the best and greatest love relationships require work, understanding, humility, empathy, and trust. When circumstances change a relationship, it's better to discuss options than pretend nothing is wrong. The deepest lesson I have learned is that love finds a way because love is the way.

I married Deborah Randolph, my present wife, in February 2003. We moved to Riverside Drive in Harlem. Debby has a master's degree in elementary education but is now happily retired. Her son, John, is just a few months older than Nairobi. As Jay Smooth, he is well known for his video blog "Ill Doctrine." A commentator at the National Museum of African American History & Culture in DC, he has been featured on many hip-hop and political outlets, including *All In* with Chris Hayes and Melissa Harris-Perry. I go to his performances and learn. He comes to my performances and learns. I'm proud of him and proud he is my stepson.

The other lesson their mothers and I passed on to our children was the importance of following one's passions. That's what Dad's tales of cross-country adventure were really about. That's what Pops showed me every day as a teacher and musician. He followed his passion. That's what he and Moms reminded me to follow when I feared I would flunk out of college as an architecture student. That's what our daughters overheard when their mothers and I were balancing tours and finances. That's what John and I talk over when he's got a new project.

Following their passions brought my children success. Having had the courage to listen to their heart, understand their talent, and discover how to share it with the world, they are immersed in the thing they love to do.

And just like me, they get better and better at it every year.

# ACKNOWLEDGMENTS

As a musician, I wish to thank my teachers. Oliver S. Coleman was my major music teacher, beginning when I was seven years old. He taught me how to sight read musical rhythmic notation and how to analyze unusual rhythmic patterns. He provided excellent preparation for understanding the more challenging scores I was about to face.

My high school band director, J. Irving Tallmadge, exposed me to the entire symphonic repertoire of percussion music literature which prepared me to succeed in college and as a professional percussionist.

My first percussion instructor at the University of Illinois, Paul W. Price, exposed me to the most difficult musical rhythmic notation. After studying with him, I could comprehend any score I encountered at the professional level. For example, the first Broadway show I ever did was *West Side Story*. No other written score was as challenging as that first one and none of them gave me any difficulty after that first exposure. Professor Price also taught me the technique of playing timpani that I have employed to this day. He exposed me to the contemporary composers who were changing the music harmonically and rhythmically from the traditional European classical era to more complex rhythmic and harmonic notation.

My associate for more than fifty years, Anton R. Reid managed Studio WIS shortly after I acquired the loft at 151 West 21st Street in the Chelsea section of Manhattan in 1967. Originally, it was just a rehearsal space used by Max Roach and several other percussionists. But it was Anton's idea to turn the studio into a performance space. During the Loft Era we gave concerts, provided musical instruction to students, and developed a series of percussion presentations. One outstanding presenter was drummer and teacher Charlie Persip. As Oliver Coleman and Paul Price had done, Charlie taught me the next thing I needed to learn: how to analyze orchestral scores and large ensemble settings. Developing this skill enriched my own playing, arranging, and composing.

I wish to thank Kirpal Gordon for his guidance. He helped me to organize my thoughts and always encouraged me through my rough periods of preparation.

I suddenly realized that I was a great-grandfather. The impressions my ancestors and elders left on me were important as I grew and matured. Kirpal has helped me pass these feelings on to my family, friends, and the young ones watching, whom we hope will have a better and more loving world in the future.

I would like to thank my archival assistant Leah Bowden for her invaluable assistance with my extensive archives. I would also like to thank Marty Khan and Helene Cann of Outward Visions Inc. for the strategic and management guidance they provide to me and WIS Percussion Theater. Inc. in helping this book become a reality.

Finally, I want to thank Laura Mitchell and Tabetha Hedrick for their assistance in getting this book to the final stages.

I wish to dedicate my story to my family: my wife Debby Randolph; my five daughters: Lynn, Leslie, Mikey, Stephanie and Nairobi; and my second wife Patricia. I wish to let them all know how much they and my deceased first wife, Mary Carmen Scott, have influenced my life and my professional career as an educator and performer. They have all helped make my accomplishments possible and given me the support I needed to make my efforts worthwhile.

I've never been able to stop trying to give all my effort to every endeavor I was engaged in. My parents and relatives prepared me to succeed and always encouraged and supported me. I sincerely feel that I was given the attitude to always try and help those I could. One of the messages that my father gave me early was to help others and not get in the way of those I could not help. This attitude has made my life comfortable. I have no regrets and no fear of the future.

I also wish to thank my brother, Frank Evans Smith, for always being at my side whenever I needed him. As we used to say, "From the cradle to the grave." I'll be here for him as long as I am able. My family is my life, and my closest friends are and always have been part of my family.

## *Enjoy this book?*

*You can make a big difference.*

Word-of-mouth is critical to an author's success. Honest reviews of this book help bring the attention of new readers. If you enjoyed this book, please take a few moments to visit your preferred online book retailer and leave a review.

## *About the Author*

Legendary percussionist, drummer, and composer Warren I. Smith entered the professional music scene at age fourteen. Rooted in the rich musical tapestry of Chicago's south side, he completed his Master of Music at the prestigious Manhattan School of Music in 1958. Fluent in mallets, tympani, and all classical techniques, his talent for maintaining parallel tracks in jazz, orchestral, Broadway, and studio music elevated the profile and appreciation of percussion in all the genres he touched.

Throughout his esteemed career, Smith's creativity and uncompromising sound graced the stages and studios alongside an impressive roster of icons, including memorable stints with Aretha Franklin, Miles Davis, and Charles Mingus. He was an original member of the experimental jazz ensemble, M'Boom, founded by Max Roach, served as the Musical Director for Janis Joplin on her iconic European tour, played alongside Nat King Cole, and even toured the United States with Barbra Streisand. Smith's contributions extended beyond his stellar performances, as he generously shared his wisdom through mentoring emerging talents and teaching at Adelphi

University and the State University of New York, College at Old Westbury.

Warren Smith's legacy transcends mere musicality. He was known in music circles as the "Do Drop In" host—a generous spirit who never turned anyone away or missed an opportunity to share sage advice and nurture friendships. His remarkable six-decade musical journey embodies a lifetime of dedication to the art of percussion and the enduring rhythm that unites us all: the human heart.

My parents Dorothea and Henry Warren Smith, Senior; Chicago, 1967, photographer unknown.

Me, my mother Dorothea and my brother Frank; Chicago, 1938, photographer unknown.

Mary and me; University of Illinois Dance, 1956, photo by Illini Studios

Me with my brother, Frank; photo by Kim Smith Penelton Campbell.

At the beach with my daughters Leslie, Lynn, Mikey, me, Steph and Robi; 2014, photo by Mary Pat Myers, M.P. Myers Photography.

My present wife Debby Randolph and me; New York, 2016, photo by Stephanie Walden.

My second wife Patricia Lucille Hall and me with our daughter Nairobi; New York, 1983, photographer unknown.

Me and the marimba; New York, 1991, photographer unknown.

My mentor Max Roach and me at my retirement party; New York, photo by Stephanie Walden.

The Warren Smith Trio: saxophonist Edith Lettner, me and saxophonist Ras Moshe; New York, 1997, photographer unknown.

Leslie Lowell Mejia's Father

Made in the USA
Middletown, DE
19 November 2023